WHAT IS A MAGICAL HOUSEHOLD?

It can be your home, whether you live in a mansion or a cold-water 5th floor walk-up. It can make coming home each day after work or school a pleasure instead of just a place to go. It can make your life happier and more fulfilling.

THE MAGICAL HOUSEHOLD recognizes that everything in the world is inherently special! Most of the time we ignore these special qualities. But sometimes we let them out. This is what we call magic—not the magic of complex rituals and expensive trappings, but the magic that is life itself.

In ***THE MAGICAL HOUSEHOLD*** you will learn to bring out the magic that is in your personal world. You will learn magic for the kitchen: alchemy. You will learn magic for the bedroom: prophetic dreams, nocturnal healings, love attraction. You will learn magic with furniture, the woodwork, the windows, and even how your beloved pets can magically improve your life.

IT'S ALL EASY, SIMPLE AND SAFE.
IT REQUIRES NOTHING MORE THAN THIS BOOK
AND WHAT YOU ALREADY HAVE IN YOUR HOME.

You will learn spells for prosperity, spells for love and spells for health. You will learn simple rituals to help purify your home and safeguard its occupants. You will learn to make your home into one where both the physical and spiritual realities are recognized and explored and where mystic rites are celebrated as a natural part of life.

IF YOU DON'T LIKE THE IDEA OF MAGIC, YOU NEED THIS BOOK! For here you will learn to simply and safely change your life and feel happier and healthier. Here you will learn ancient secrets for security and contentment. Here you will learn to help make your life into what you want it to be.

IF YOU LIKE MAGIC, YOU NEED THIS BOOK! Here you will discover traditional secrets long hidden from the masses. Here you will discover that magic can be more than just something you occasionally do. It can be part of your life—24 hours a day. Here you will find kitchen magic, door magic, indoor garden magic, bath magic, cosmetic magic, magic with pets, even magic with the garage! Here you will learn to do protection spells and make household guardians.

THE MAGICAL HOUSEHOLD can be yours. It doesn't take years to improve your life, it just takes your desire to achieve the best for your life and loved ones. Why don't you start now?

About the Authors

DAVID HARRINGTON lives in Chula Vista, California and has a long-time interest in the mysteries of household magic. He is currently working on a new project for Llewellyn Publications. This is his first book.

SCOTT CUNNINGHAM continues to write full-time in the occult and New Age fields. His latest projects include a work investigating the magical aspects of food and a guide to ancient Sumerian and Babylonian magic.

To Write to the Authors

We cannot guarantee that every letter written to the authors can be answered, but all will be forwarded. Both the authors and the publisher appreciate hearing from readers, learning of your enjoyment and benefit from this book. Llewellyn also publishes a bimonthly news magazine with news and reviews of practical esoteric studies and articles helpful to the student, and some readers' questions and comments to the authors may be answered through this magazine's columns if permission to do is included in the original letter. The authors sometimes participate in seminars and workshops, and dates and places are announced in *The Llewellyn New Times*. To write to the authors, or to ask a question, write to:

Scott Cunningham/David Harrington
c/o THE LLEWELLYN NEW TIMES
P.O. Box 64383-124, St. Paul, MN 55164-0383, U.S.A.

Please enclose a self-addressed, stamped envelope for reply, or $1.00 to cover costs.

About Llewellyn's Practical Magick Series

To some people, the idea that "Magick" is *practical* comes as a suprise.

It shouldn't. The entire basis for Magick is to exercise influence over one's environment. While Magick is also, and properly so, concerned with spiritual growth and psychological transformation, even the spiritual life must rest firmly on material foundations.

The material world and the psychic are intertwined, and it is this very fact that establishes the Magickal Link: that the psychic can as easily influence the material as vice versa.

Magick can, and should, be used in one's daily life for better living! Each of us has been given Mind and Body, and surely we are under Spiritual obligation to make full usage of these wonderful gifts. Mind and Body work together, and Magick is simply the extension of this interaction into dimensions beyond the limits normally conceived. That's why we commonly talk of the "super-normal" in connection with domain of Magick.

The Body is alive, and all Life is an expression of the Divine. There is God-power in the Body and in the Earth, just as there is in Mind and Spirit. With Love and Will, we use Mind to link these aspects of Divinity together to bring about change.

With Magick we increase the flow of Divinity in our lives and in the world around us. We add to the beauty of it all—for to work Magick we must work in harmony with the Laws of Nature and of the Psyche. *Magick is the flowering of the Human Potential.*

Practical Magick is concerned with the Craft of Living well and in harmony with Nature, and with the Magick of the Earth, in the things of the Earth, in the seasons and cycles and in the things we make with hand and Mind.

OTHER BOOKS BY SCOTT CUNNINGHAM

Magical Herbalism, 1982 (Llewellyn)
Earth Power, 1983 (Llewellyn)
Cunningham's Encyclopedia of Magical Herbs, 1985 (Llewellyn)
The Magic of Incense, Oils and Brews, 1986 (Llewellyn)
Cunningham's Encyclopedia of Crystal, Gem and Metal Magic,
    1987 (Llewellyn)

Forthcoming:
Wicca
Huna Magic

and additional titles dealing with practical, Nature-related magic.

Llewellyn's Practical Magick Series

The Magical Household

Empower Your Home With Love, Protection, Health and Happiness

Scott Cunningham
and
David Harrington

1988
Llewellyn Publications
St. Paul, Minnesota 55164-0383, U.S.A.

International Standard Book Number: 0-87542-124-5
Library of Congress Catalog Number: 87-45740

First Edition, 1987
First Printing, 1987
Second Printing, 1987
Third Printing, 1988

Library of Congress Cataloging-in-Publications Data

Cunningham, Scott, 1956—
    The magical household.

    (Llewellyn's practical magick series)
    Bibliography: p.
    1. Magic.   2. Household—Miscellanea.   I. Harrington, David.
    II Title.   III. Series
    BF1623.H67C86   1987   133.4'3   87-4570
    ISBN 0-87542-124-5

Cover Painting by Robin Wood
Illustrations by Martin Cannon
Book Design by Terry Buske

Produced by Llewellyn Publications
Typography and Art property of Chester-Kent, Inc.

Published by
LLEWELLYN PUBLICATIONS
A Division of Chester-Kent, Inc.
P.O. Box 64383
St. Paul, MN 55164-0383, U.S.A.
Printed in the United States of America

DEDICATION

to friendship

ACKNOWLEDGEMENTS

We thank Morgana of Hawaii for graciously allowing us to include some of her spells and rituals in this book. *Mahalo nui loa.*

The authors also wish to express their appreciation to all the individuals who shared their own household magic with them.

TABLE OF CONTENTS

PREFACE

Back in 1982, David Harrington suggested I write a book about the magical aspects of the home (the original working title was "The Witch's Cottage"). I thought it was a great idea. Though much has been written concerning magic over the past 15 years, little has been said regarding the home and its mystical qualities. Just as *Magical Herbalism* was the result of a lack of published magical herbals, household magic seemed an ideal topic for a book.

I soon realized that, while I had lived a magical life for well over a decade, writing a book about household magic wasn't an easy task. David and I discussed the idea for some time, agreeing that it was an interesting project, but I couldn't find the secret to transforming it into a book.

One day, when David asked me about "The Witch's Cottage" again, I told him if he wanted to see that book, he should either write it himself or help me write it.

We started on New Year's Eve. In the following months, while I worked at what was to become *Cunningham's Encyclopedia of Magical Herbs*, we scribbled ideas, impressions and rituals on paper. Long, rainy afternoons spent at the downtown San Diego public library reading up on ancient house customs merged with nights when we ransacked our personal libraries to fill in the gaps in our knowledge.

Over the next two years, we finally put together a book of sorts. It wasn't what either of us had envisioned, so I continued to rewrite, edit and expand the information, with David providing witty comments and erudite criticism on each draft.

Soon, *Earth Power* and the *Encyclopedia* were published. For several months, I set *The Magical Household* (the second working title) aside and concentrated on finishing other projects—*The Magic of Incense,* an as-yet-untitled (but nearly finished) book on Wicca, and various novels. As soon as a lull occurred in late 1985, I set out to smooth the rough edges and complete this book.

The Magical Household is the product of two people's dreams, imaginations, experiences and studies. Though I put most of the words down on paper, the book is as fully David's as it is mine, for it grew out of his love for the magical home and for the arcane ways of past ages.

So, welcome, finally, to this "house between pages." Settle back in your chair and sip herbal tea as you explore the place. It is my fondest hope—as I'm sure it is David's—that you feel at home while reading this book within your own magical household.

Scott Cunningham
San Diego, 1987

INTRODUCTION

The Witch's cottage lay at the edge of the forest, where luxuriant brush, wild herbs and brambles formed a dense maze among ancient oaks, pines and twisted hawthorns.

A mossy cobblestone path meandered through patches of green and gray foliage, while surrounding the herbs, more familiar blossoms of rainbow hues nodded gently in the rose-scented breeze.

A wooden bucket swung in the stone well, which was amply guarded against contamination by the deeply carved stars and spirals surrounding it.

A dragon, one clawed paw upraised, flew above the house, twisting with the wind as it rode a wrought-iron arrow. The weathervane guided the enchantress living in the cottage in matters ranging from timing spells to divining the future.

Beside the round-topped cottage door, a rowan tree flourished, brightly sprinkled with bunches of scarlet berries. Smoke snaked from the spiral brick chimney, sending hints of applewood swirling through the mists.

Inside the iron-wrapped door, the cottage was warm, inviting—laden with exotic scents and the hum of beneficent forces.

Above the door, a horseshoe—nailed points upward—allowed only good to enter the home. Across the room, pungent herbs to be used later in potions and brews hung drying from the rafters while roots lay close to the chimney.

Horse-brasses reflected the glowing fire along the brick wall facing the hearth. Crescent moons, stars, griffins and blazing suns—originally designed to guard horses— added their magic to the cottage.

In each room and corner of the home, magic abounded. Food was blessed before cooking; beds were situated East-to-West; a broom lay on the floor before the door; a bag of herbs hung from the chair on a red cord—no part of the Witch's cottage was left unblessed or unguarded by the wonders of magic.

Life within the home was by its nature arcane. A student of magic, the woman who owned the house saw magic at work in her life, from rising with the Sun until falling exhausted after a day of spinning and weaving, cooking, herb harvesting, cleaning, contemplating, blessing and spell-casting.

Such might have been the magical household of the past, when healing charms, spells and potions, home spirits, herb magic, Witches, magicians and ghosts were accepted as real. No part of everyday life was untouched by the unseen. All aspects of existence were suffused with magical tradition and ceremony.

The structures that housed and protected these early peoples were more than bricks, reeds or logs. Houses were psychic centers, pools of protective energy in which families lived to guard themselves against the dangers of everyday life.

The house was also a shrine to the deity of life itself. Its roof and walls served as a shield from the effects of the elements (both physical and magical) and held in the home's luck, spirit or energy, while its door guarded against unwanted intrusions. The house sustained life; it was sacred and powerful.

Today, however, we've lost our mystic reverence for our homes. Even those of us called toward the forgotten ways of magic often fail to see its powers and influences at work in our everyday lives.

Fortunately, it isn't difficult to create a magical household, one patterned after ancient ritual and magical ways. You needn't move to a forest cottage or a damp mountaintop castle. Your own home will do, whether it's a cramped studio apartment or a sprawling, triple-wide mobile home, for a magical household is one in which the home is attuned with the rhythms and energies of nature.

You also needn't become a Witch or magician to bring your home in tune with ageless magic, nor must you change your religious affiliation, if any.

If you live with others—family, mate or roomies—they can participate in household magic or not, as they choose.

If, while reading this book, something strikes your fancy, try it out. This isn't an academic history of mystic cottages, but a practical guide to transforming your life and living space.

With a minimum of time and imagination, the most modern home can be brought into line with the charmed cottages of yesterday. To do this, we needn't turn our backs on our world nor slavishly adhere to ancient modes of thinking.

However, we can take clues from the past and create an atmosphere of harmony, safety, spirituality, security and romance in our homes. The benefits—a happier existence, protection against thieves, improved health, restful sleep, satisfying spiritual experiences and a perfect environment for positive magic—far outweigh the minor expenditures of time, money and energy.

Creating a secure, magical environment in our homes means fashioning an escape from the all-too-physical reality of a world that has turned its back on the spiritual side of life. The home can be transformed into a meditative cocoon of positive energy that provides refuge from the stormy atmosphere of our world.

But the magical home isn't just a fortress. It is one in which the magic of life is recognized and celebrated through timeless rites and spells. Even if we don't live in a seventeenth-century English cottage, a reed hut perched on the banks of the Euphrates river or a hollow tree in the New Forest, we can create a place in which both physical and spiritual realities are acknowledged and explored, filling our lives with wonder and excitement.

We are in control of our home environment. Just as the magician uses wand and spell to change the world, so can we transform our nondescript apartments and tract homes into satisfying versions of the magical dwellings of yore. We can do this by taking ideas from the past and applying them today so that our lives will be filled with tomorrows of enchantment.

A NOTE ON MAGIC

This book is about magic—everyday magic that is designed to improve our lives and homes. You needn't be an expert on magic to follow these simple rites and spells; the only advanced technique required of you is the art of *visualization.*

Visualization is the act of controlled imagination. If you can call up in your mind a picture of your best friend's face or a flag flapping in the breeze, you can visualize.

In magic, visualizations are used to direct and control magical energies. Basically, the spell-caster creates a visual image of the spell's desired goal, whether it be perfect health, a safe house or a guarded pet. As you will see clearly in the pages ahead, magic, once mastered, is easy to perform.

Though visualization is the basis of all spells (which are designed—or should be designed—to help us maintain our visualizations), it is simply a tool which should be properly used. It must be real in the mind of the spell-caster so that it allows him or her to raise, concentrate and send forth energy to accomplish the spell.

Perhaps when visualizing, you'll find that you're doing everything right, but that you don't *feel* anything. This is common, for we haven't been trained to acknowledge—let alone utilize—our magical abilities. Keep practicing, however, for your spells can "take" even if you're not the most experienced natural magician.

Even when your spells are effective, magic won't usually sparkle before your very eyes. The test of magic's success is time, not immediate eye-popping results.

So what is this magic power? You can feel it for yourself by rubbing your palms together briskly for 10 seconds, then holding them a few inches apart. Sense the energy passing through them, the warm tingle in your palms. This is the power raised and used in magic. It comes from within and is perfectly natural.

Since this isn't a book on magical technique or philosophy, I'll limit the "how-to" instructions to topics actually discussed in the text. If you decide you'd like to pursue a course of magical studies, some of the books listed in the bibliography should prove to be fine starting points.

1   House Lore

There have always been magical households.

The earliest dwellings, as every schoolchild knows, were caves. Prehistoric humans moved into uninhabited caverns and set up housekeeping. Where caves were scarce or unavailable, Paleolithic peoples fashioned tents or dug underground homes. To guard against the effects of nasty weather, these dwellings were carefully sited, often along river valleys under overhanging cliffs.

Tents were stitched together from skins (ancient needles have been found), while more substantial "houses" were dug into the earth and roofed with hide and chunks of turf.

Burning bones and wood for heat, these early peoples were sheltered, housed and reasonably safe. Food could be found all around them.

We can't know what Paleolithic peoples thought of the world or their place in it, nor can we determine their religious or spiritual ideas. Some archaeologists have formulated guesses based on cave paintings, carvings and statuettes concerning the earliest religious and magical thinking, but these remain mere speculation.

Still, those early peoples must have desired many of the same things we do—companionship, security, food, entertainment, sex and contentment. Although their homes lacked solar-heating units, steel girders and three-car garages, they served the same function ours do today: protection.

These earlier peoples saw their homes as shields against spirits and unseen forces—the powers that seemingly propel the Sun and Moon across the sky, cause fire to flash in the night and deliver warmth after the killing chills of winter.

As such, the house was imbued with magical qualities, as was most of life. Having enabled these early peoples to live through the last great ice age, the house assumed a sacred character. In the Western world, vestiges of this mystic aura lingered until World War II, when many rural customs were forever destroyed. But in the East and isolated parts of the West, the home still retains a trace of its magical heritage.

The earliest religious rites probably occurred in the communal home. Once household spirits and deities were worshiped, home religious practices were modified to include reverence for the house spirit. The most famous of these spirits are the *Lares* of the Romans. The Lares were both household and family deities. They were consulted on daily family affairs and given offerings of flour and salt.

So the home was the center of life, not only in this world but in the spiritual world as well. Every home was a temple.

When homes were built, sacrifices were made to appease these early household goddesses and gods. These sacrifices included fruits and grains, animals, and newly laid fertile eggs. (The eggs were often substituted for living flesh, which earlier peoples throughout the world once deemed the fittest offering to deity. The egg was built into the house or broken over its foundation to bless it with life-giving energy.)

The home has always been guarded magically. The Saxons, for example, placed antlers at the ends and peaks of their roofs to drive away evil. (This custom is faintly echoed in the now-diminishing use of roof finials.) During medieval times,

iron was used to safeguard the house. Forkheads, lengths of chain, broken scythes and swords were neatly arranged under house foundations to halt the entrance of evil magic. Later, brooms were walled up for protective purposes.

This is an important concept—that of "evil" magic. Only one kind of power is used in magic, although it may be raised in a number of ways. Magic, the use of this power, is of two types: *positive* and *negative*.

Two hundred years ago, and even more recently, everyone performed magic as a part of everyday life. Batter was stirred sunwise, silver was turned at the sight of the New Moon and babies were guarded in their cradles with garlic. Most superstitions are remnants of such old magical acts.

These early peoples didn't stop the flow of *all* magic into their homes, just the real or imagined "evil" type. They invited the positive, beneficial magic to enter and then cast spells inside the home to create a stronger spirit or essence. Today, a magical household isn't simply one that is guarded against negative magic; it is a place where positive magic blossoms.

Today, the home has lost most of its magical qualities. In China, however, homes are still designed and sited according to ancient magical tradition. No one built homes in earlier times without first consulting the *Feng Shui* man, an expert on natural Earth configurations (mountains, plains, valleys, rivers, rocks, bays) as well as buildings and their magical properties.

For example, an ideal house is built in a u-shape, with the ocean in front of it and a mountain behind. Roads must never run straight toward the house, for energy (*ch'i*) travels along straight roads. Those living within such a house would literally burn out from the excessive energy. A right-angled turn in the road reduces the energy flow into the home, protecting it and its inhabitants.

The Chinese also revere five household gods or spirits

who reside in every home: *Men*, God of Doors; *Hu*, God of the Windows; *Chin Chu'an*, God of the Well; *Chung Liu*, God of the Eaves; and *Tsao Chun*, God of the Hearth and Kitchen Stove, who safeguards the entire house and watches over the conduct of those occupying it.

Unfortunately, China's recent race to learn and utilize Western technology may soon end the old traditions in the homeland. The young are no longer interested in the ways of their grandparents. Though now outlawed in China, *Feng Shui* is apparently flourishing in Hong Kong.

Numerous curious traditions regarding the house and its construction have survived. In the Middle East, for example, a house must have an even number of rafters or it is said to be unlucky. In Thailand, on the other hand, houses usually possess an odd number of doors, windows, rooms and stairs in the belief that an even number would allow earthquakes to shake down the house.

In Hawaii, it was believed that a home built beside a taller adjacent dwelling would have its good fortune drained away by its taller neighbor. Thus, anyone who lived in the house would suffer the consequences.

In the Ozarks in recent times, old-time hill men utilized a few boards from an old building in the construction of a new home. If this wasn't done, ill fortune, sickness or even death was said to fall on the people who lived in the house.

Perhaps the most colorful remnants of home magic in the United States today are the Pennsylvania Dutch hex symbols. These colorful round signs—still to be seen freshly painted on farm houses and barns in southeastern Pennsylvania—have nothing to do with either hexes or Holland. The word "Dutch" is a corruption of *Deutsch*, or German. Many of the persecuted refugees who settled in Pennsylvania came from Germany.

The symbols, or signs, were once known as *sechs*, which is German for six. Perhaps they were called this because they often contain six-pointed stars. At some point, the word changed from *sechs* to hex (derived from the German word for Witch). Today we know these symbols as Pennsylvania Dutch hex symbols.

Emblazoned on huge barns and sturdy, clean houses, hex signs continue to spread their spells. They are a curious combination of magic and religion—a guard for the home and farm as well as a graphic celebration of nature and the divine.

Raindrops, stars, oak leaves and acorns, four-leaf clovers, hearts, tulips and doves, lilies and abstract geometrical patterns are common design elements. Vivid colors are also used for their mystical properties. Green brings abundance, happiness, luck and prosperity to the home. Blue signifies spiritual love, protection, beauty and truth. Brown invokes earthiness and sensual pleasure, while white represents purity, joy and protection. Red brings love and liberty. Combinations of red, blue and yellow guard against sickness and spells.

According to one tradition, seven hex signs on a single building guard it against wicked spells, fire, lightning, floods and other natural disasters. Though hex signs are sometimes painted or hung on buildings, they are most often used within the home. Specific signs are hung over the bed or in the main room to attract love, health and wealth to the home's occupants. Whatever their origins, hex symbols are colorful reminders that house magic is still alive today.

A current example of old lore regarding the house concerns the liberal application of white paint or stickers to windows of homes and buildings still under construction. This was originally done so that evil spirits, frightened or magically blocked by the white paint, couldn't fly in through the closed windows and take up residence before the house was finished and its tenants had moved in.

The magical nature of our homes hasn't changed significantly throughout our evolution from cave-dwellers to apartment renters. A Paleolithic woman, snuggling beneath skins in the comparative warmth and safety of her primitive home, may not have enjoyed the gifts that millenia of civilization have given us. She did, however, possess an affinity for the natural world that we have lost.

Safe beneath the skins, the fire crackling at her feet and family members surrounding her, she must have dropped off into the realm of dreams secure in her magical home—guarded against the spirits that rode the winds and the savage tribe that lived beyond the next mountain range.

Can we do the same?

2   The Hearth

Before the days of central heating, the hearth was the center of the home—the protectant of life during cold winter months, the heat for cooking all meals and the gathering place of the household. Indeed, since primitive times, the hearth has been the most popular, as well as the warmest, place in the home.

Today, fireplaces are rarities in new homes and apartments. The necessity of the past is fast becoming a present-day luxury. Fireplaces often increase house prices and are seldom used. In old homes, fireplaces are often in such poor shape they're nothing more than fire hazards.

Fire has a special attraction for many of us. Within its hypnotic movements and fragrant smoke lie the origins of many religions. Fire was once supernatural—a divine substance stolen from the deities. It can be traced to early religious and magical rites around the world, and flames are still found on the altars of many established religions.

Magically, Fire is the element of transformation; through its work, true change occurs. It is seen as kin to the spark of life that exists within all things. It can be destructive, true, but it also creates. Change can occur only with the destruction of the old. The very nature of destruction is creation.

In the days before matches were readily available, the

fire in the house was never allowed to die, except on ritual occasions. At night, the coals were banked up so that new flames would spring from them in the morning. It was considered unfortunate if the household fire extinguished itself. When this occurred, hot coals had to be borrowed from neighbors. If the coals died while being transported, it was a sign that the family was in for a troubled future.

In this age of microwave ovens and electric ranges, it is difficult to imagine the importance of fire only a half-century ago. As late as the 1960's, Scott's grandmother stoked her cast-iron stove with wood early in the morning, just before sunrise, to warm the farmhouse's kitchen and brew coffee.

At night, before the advent of radio and television—when few could read or write—the household would gather before the fire and share stories of times past, preserving family lore and educating the young. All would watch the flames for omens of the future.

Fire and magic have been associated for eons. Both have incredible potential for good and evil; thus, both must be handled with care.

The fireplace can be viewed as the heart of the house as well as an altar to the forces of nature that have shaped our world and with which we transform our lives. We need not worship fire to enjoy and utilize it, but the fireplace is often given special attention in magical households.

Upon moving into a new house, for example, magicians who work with fire often restore the fireplace to its former state of glory. Bricks are scrubbed to remove years of smoke deposits, andirons (the guardians of the fireplace) are polished and ashes are swept up and safely deposited, for they are considered things of power.

Because the chimney is a magical entrance to the house (witness the confused ideas of Santa Claus descending the chimney and Witches flying up it astride brooms), it has long been magically guarded. Plants are often utilized in such rites—perhaps not surprisingly, since they are consumed within the fireplace. Olive branches hung on the chimney keep it secure and serve to deflect lightning strikes. Pine needles scattered in the fireplace or cypress lain on the hearth work similarly for the fireplace as a whole. A lady's-slipper orchid hung from the chimney prevents outsiders from casting spells against the home's inhabitants.

Crossing the poker and tongs before the fireplace prevents sparks from popping out onto the floor and magically cancels any negative energies that might float down through it. A horseshoe lain in the ashes guards the entire fireplace. A jar of salt on the hearth comes in handy in times of argument, tension or danger of any kind. Simply throw a pinch on the flames, and its cleansing powers, when released by the flames, bless your home.

Three circles drawn with white chalk on the hearth ban evil from entering. This was commonly done in England until quite recently and may continue today.

A new hearthstone is blessed by covering it with salt and sketching a pentagram (a five-pointed star) on it. A pentagram periodically redrawn in the ashes renews the spell.

The starting of fires, once a rare event, is filled with lore. According to tradition, fires must have at least 13 sticks to burn properly. It is considered unwise to look directly at a fire while lighting it, as if the process were sacred and not meant for human eyes. Doing so will not only hinder the fire's burning but may also bring bad luck to the entire household.

Untold thousands of spells have been cast by firelight or within the fireplace itself. When the fireplace was cold, Witches or magicians raked the ashes into a circle on the hearth, then cast spells within this circle. A blazing fire is useful for simple transformative spells, such as those in which dragon's blood, rosemary or rose petals are cast into the flames. Such actions, accompanied by the proper visualizations, bring love to the spell-maker. Nettles thrown into

the fire conquer fear, while vervain dispels the pangs of unre-
quited love.

Wish magic is easily performed at the fire. If you wish for
something, poke the flames for 13 minutes with the poker,
visualizing your wish.

At one time, women who had lost their men to rivals
would calmly sit before the fire on seven consecutive nights,
casting salt into its heat in an attempt to draw their husbands
back home.

The type of wood burned within the fireplace can affect
spells immensely. Oak is burned during healing magic, when
someone in the home is sick. This helps to "draw off" the illness, aids in recovery and guards the rest of the household
from contracting the sickness. Applewood is burned before
lovers meet at home, or as an adjunct to love spells. Ash logs
promote energy, pine brings money into the home and
juniper offers protection.

Perhaps one of the most common magical rites performed near the fireplace is fire-gazing. Some old adepts
claim that gazing into the fire at midnight produces the best
results, especially for seeing visions of the future.

If you wish to summon the faces of absent friends, sit to
the left of a fire, stir the logs with the poker in your right hand
and watch the embers. Their faces will appear in the coals.

Fire-gazing is a wonderful pastime, and with practice
can help develop one's psychic powers to a fine pitch. If you
have an affinity for fire, you may wish to try this.

Sit comfortably before the fire. Wait until the flames have
died down and a sea of glowing reddish-orange coals stretches
out before you. Still your mind. Gaze with half-opened eyes
at the constantly pulsating and changing embers. Don't *will*
yourself to see pictures or visions; relax and allow yourself the
experience. If symbols appear, interpret them according to
your own intuition.

Dion Fortune, in her classic magical novel *The Sea*

Priestess, preserved the custom of fire-gazing in a blaze made of sandalwood, juniper and cedar logs. A simpler method consists of combining ground sandalwood, cedar and juniper and tossing this mixture onto the coals just prior to gazing.

Fireplaces are often prognosticators of home life. Sparks scattering in showers of gold from the chimney signal money in the future of the observer. A fire sparkling brightly is a sign of rain. A blue flame in the fire—or a mass of blue flames—indicates a snap of cold weather coming. If the fire catches and lights quickly when you set it, expect unexpected company.

The lazy housekeeper who allows ashes to pile up beyond reasonable amounts should remove them quickly, for this is a sign that the rent will increase.

In magical thought, ashes are sacred. Scattering them over the house roof protects it from damage caused by lightning. Strewing ashes in dark corners of the house protects it from burning down, while carrying a small bag of ashes wards off evil, accidents and disease.

The ashes from magical fires or spells, or even normal ashes, are used in a wide variety of spells related to the element of Fire. Ashes can be used to increase courage (when carried in a red cloth sack), energy (when smeared on the body in a tiny area) and healing (when placed around a purple candle).

Ashes not used in spells are often buried in isolated places, not only out of respect to the old fire deities but also to seal any spells with which they may have been involved.

Just 100 years ago, every fireplace had a cauldron. If its three legs left a print in the ashes, the ashes were quickly stirred because "evil spirits" could use the imprints as the cauldron itself and cause mischief to the genuine article.

The importance of the fireplace cannot be overstated. One sign of a contented home is a cat sitting on the hearth. Some say you'll never have good luck in a new house until the chimney has been blackened with smoke.

Sitting before a fire on a cold winter's night, sipping hot cider and gazing into its flames and embers, directly aligns us with peoples of the past who viewed fire and religion as one. If you have a fireplace, use it, for it is a tremendous boon to the magical household.

Smoke rising from a chimney traditionally denotes a happy life for those residing in the house.

May your chimney always be smoking!

3   Thresholds of Power

The door has long captured the imagination of poets, mystics and magicians. It is symbolic, often appearing in dreams and nightmares. What lies behind the door? What strange creatures, fabulous wonderlands, hidden dangers?

While more pedestrian, windows have their magical properties and lore as well. If they are the eyes of a home, the door is its mouth. Both possess special powers, and both are generally blessed to prevent the entrance of unfriendly energies into the home.

A door isn't much—a flat piece of wood, two knobs, three hinges, some hardware. But doors are entrances into other dimensions. In form, they echo the trilithons of Stonehenge and other European megalithic structures: two upright stones with a third resting on top, creating a threshold of power.

Doors are entrances to buildings as well as exits from them; therefore, they are often seen as gateways to other worlds. They also serve as protective devices that bar the dangerous from entering. Because of this, the door and all its parts (lintel, posts, threshold, keys) have assumed magical, almost sacral qualities.

Many of the rites associated with doors are protective

15

in nature. Hanging a gourd on both sides of the outside of a door will ward off unwanted negativity, as will a piece of bamboo or a wreath of leaves and thorns placed over it. A circle chalked on the door bars ghosts from entering; garlic or dill suspended over the front door repels those who are ill-disposed or envious of you from gaining entrance; and a bag of salt or bells hung from the knob will set demons to flight.

Other spells favored to guard the home from the entrance of evil include: placing two crossed needles under the doormat; painting the door blue, a sacred color; sprinkling mustard seeds or ground dragon's blood on the doorsill; and hammering three nails in the shape of a triangle (one point up) on the outside of the front door.

Specific herbs are grown on the porch to further protect the home. Ferns, lilies, marigolds and juniper are grown there in pots. An old sock filled with salt, sage, mullein, tansy and any other protective herbs can be buried beneath the front porch to keep ghosts from the home. A box of holed stones or a knife beneath the porch are similarly potent magical protectants.

The door also functions as an ideal place for inviting certain energies or attributes into your home. Five shiny pennies placed beneath the porch will bring the household money and love, for instance, and a bit of food buried there ensures that you won't know hunger.

If you wish to see a ghost, the doorway is an ideal place to practice, according to ancient tradition. At dusk or midnight, stand at any door in the dark, looking into another room. With the door half-opened, lay your cheek against it and peer just past its edge. If you persevere, you may see spirits and strange shapes. Why? Because the door is an entrance to other worlds.

If you wish to be rid of ghosts, they can be exorcised simply by slamming a door several times in succession. The

ghosts get caught between the door and the frame and will soon have enough of the torture and leave. If you enjoy ghosts, however, don't slam doors!

If you're the type that never closes a door, you may want to start doing so. Legend says that he or she who never shuts a door will never own a house. This is probably connected with the idea that if a house's doors are left open, power "leaks out."

Keys have their own special brand of magic and were of enormous importance in ancient religion. Hecate held the keys of the universe; Janus, a Roman God of Doors, was quite often seen holding keys; and ancient priestesses and priests held keys to symbolize potent magical connection with their deities.

Keys are phallic symbols, representing the masculine principle, but they also represent wisdom, attainment of higher levels of consciousness and magical protection.

There are dozens of key spells from which to choose if you fancy them. These include such simple spells as wearing a small key (*not* carrying one) to find wisdom and placing an old iron key beneath the mattress to help in matters of sexual impotence. Other spells, such as the following one, are more complex.

Obtain as many old keys as you have doors in your home. Moving slowly through your house, take a key, touch it to the door, and repeat this until each key has touched one door. While doing say each time:

> *Lock out thieves in the night,*
> *Lock out thieves in the light,*
> *Lock out thieves out of sight.*

Once this has been repeated for each key, tie them all together with red ribbon and hang them over the front door as a magically potent decoration. Remember: visualize!

As stated earlier, keys can be carried or used for specific purposes. A gold key guards against the evil eye; three keys on a chain will bring health, wealth and love; a key slipped down the back is said to relieve a headache or halt a nosebleed; and any key carried will bring luck, so long as it doesn't fit any lock you possess.

A key placed in a cradle will "lock" the baby home so that it can't be stolen by fairies (though this isn't much of a problem today). A door key placed upside down near the bed will banish nightmares and ensure a peaceful sleep, while small keys can be placed near a pet's home to safeguard it. Wearing a key will promote fertility and conception, and if you wish to discover a secret, wear a key.

Windows are simply doors without keys. The earliest windows were slits in the walls designed to let fresh air into the home and to vent smoke. Wind whistled through them, and firelight from within the house was visible in them. Not surprisingly, window means "wind's eye."

Like doors, windows were viewed with magical awe and were protected. Pentagrams were (and still are) carved or chalked onto windows; hanging a thick white curtain blocks Sun and negativity; small white pebbles, fragments of glass and seashells are placed on the sill, as is a large red tomato; and a ball of green grass is suspended before the window to drive away evil influences.

Washing your windows with ammonia or vinegar not only cleans them but also invites the powers of the wind to bless your home.

Stained-glass windows are magically effective in driving away evil, for the intricate designs and various colors of glass set up cleansing vibrations. The patterns of these windows should be chosen with care so that they blend with the rest of the home. When sunlight shines fully through stained glass, casting beams of color-charged light into the room and forming brilliantly hued pools on the floor, magic is indeed at work!

A similar practice consists of hanging leaded crystal points or faceted spheres in the windows so that the sunlight is broken into hundreds of tiny rainbows.

Round windows, a favorite of house designers in Hawaii and the Far East, are considered to be protective to the home. They are known as "moon windows."

If you move into a new home, try working this spell (which is also effective when you are sleeping in any room for the first time): Before falling asleep, count the panes of glass in the room's windows. Then strongly visualize a wish and doze off.

And finally, if your luck has been rotten and you want to change it, scatter salt on your window sills and then take further steps to improve your luck.

4   Furnishings

Furniture possesses its own influences and lore. Choosing furnishings carefully, or arranging them to follow ancient principles, can make life within the home more harmonious, productive and loving.

First, the floor. You can install carpeting, but why not consider investing in a few area rugs? Colorful, handwoven rugs lend an air of mystery and luxury to the home. Whether loomed in Peru, Tunisia, China, the Middle East or the American Southwest, rugs have long been artifacts of magic.

The rugs that lie on your floors are kin to the flying carpets of Arabic folk magic. The very process by which a rug is created seems to indicate a link with the forces of nature—the repetitious movements of the hands, the shuttle shifting back and forth, the meshing of threads, the rug slowly building up as if by magic. Even the colors, pattern and shape possess hidden influences.

Some rug patterns are traditional, others are centuries old or modern adaptations. Some incorporate magical symbols associated with the beliefs and customs of the rug's country of origin. Colors, too, are used for their symbolic and magical meanings.

21

A rug's shape denotes its character, and, therefore, the sort of influence it will have in a home. Round rugs, symbolic of spirituality as well as peace, are best used in quiet rooms such as the bedroom, living room, dining room and meditation or temple room.

Square or rectangular rugs represent the material world, intellect and technology. These are best suited for offices, dens, libraries and entryways.

Oval rugs, which contain within their shapes the cosmic egg (the essence of all that exists), work well throughout the home.

If you study most handloomed rugs closely, you'll find minor imperfections in the weave or design. For example, a wide band of color around the rug's interior might be solid except for a small, inch-long section. This isn't a mistake; it is intentional. Many weavers leave these seeming imperfections in their work as magical "trap doors." If, while working on the piece, the weaver was upset, depressed or ill, such energies could be woven into the rug and ultimately transferred to its final owner. Therefore, these obvious deviations from the pattern allow such negative (and unavoidable) energies to leave the rug.

There is another reason for such "flaws." In earlier times, anything nearing perfection invited envy and courted disaster from the gods, who didn't care for human perfection. Jealous looks or even open admiration could land the dreaded "evil eye" on the rug. This evil eye—a look supposedly able to transfer negative energies between the viewer and the object or person viewed—was so feared that nothing was made precisely to the pattern.

There are a few magical practices concerning rugs that you can follow. For example, if you are low on money and luck, try tucking a bit of dried Irish moss (seaweed) under your rugs. This may perk up your financial scene.

If you accidentally turn a rug wrong-side up, don't

change it. Everyone who walks over it while it remains in this condition will be suffused with blessings.

Never tack down rugs or carpeting until after you've washed the floor. Cleaning the floor sweeps away stagnant energies and brings them into alignment with the house's positive energy flow.

Before vacuuming rugs and carpets, sprinkle sweet-smelling herbs onto them. This will leave a fresh scent on the carpet. Lavender is fine for this.

To purify rugs, sprinkle them with salt and beat them outside, or use a vacuum cleaner.

A particularly special rug, usually one that is round or oval, can be used solely for magic. Some people sew, paint or embroider magical symbols on such a rug and then lay it on the floor during rituals. The rug is used to mark out a circle of power in which magic and ritual will be made.

In past times, most chairs, stools, clocks and other household items were marked with protective symbols—usually sun wheels, pentagrams or equal-armed crosses—to guard them against bewitchment.

And the clock—what an extraordinary tool the clock is! Whether made of water and buckets, candles burning past specified markings, sundials or cogged and geared mechanical devices, how magical it must have seemed to earlier peoples. In today's world of digital and LED clocks, we've forgotten the old magic of a huge grandfather clock ticking away in the living room at night, or the school-sized model that solemnly kept watch over the dinner table.

In the days when clocks had to be wound and their accuracy was rather lax, the sudden stoppage of the familiar ticking was cause for alarm, as was an eerie thirteenth chime in the dead of night. If the clock had been wound sufficiently and had never before misstruck, it was plain—the clock must be enchanted! Fortunately, it was easy to lift the spell. The clock was carried out the back door and in through the front, after which it was supposed to work perfectly again.

It has long been believed that if you are wishing for something as a clock chimes, your wish will come true. Of course, you could stand next to the Seth-Thomas and wait for the right moment, but that isn't quite the same thing.

If you ever think you've fallen victim to a hex or curse, simply crawl under a six-legged table to break the spell. Why? Because the table is an altar, and by climbing beneath it, you petition the divine's blessings and aid in lifting the spell.

The woods have their own magical powers and influences, and your chairs, couches, desks and stools—in fact, all your wooden furniture—contain the energies of the woods from which they were made.

Ebony, for example, is a wood of magical power and protection. Furniture made from it is ideal for rooms in which magic is frequently performed.

Following is a list of woods and their magical influences. You might keep these in mind when purchasing new furniture.

Ebony: magical power, protection
Oak: strength, luck, health, protection
Pine: money, exorcism, healing
Redwood: longevity
Cherry: love
Teak: riches
Cedar: healing, longevity, purification, protection
Maple: love, money
Mahogany: protection against lightning
Rattan: luck, strength
Walnut: health

If you plan to redecorate soon, you might wish to wait

until the New Moon. Moving furniture at that time grants good fortune to the mover.

Mirrors are the perfect example of an everyday household furnishing fraught with superstition. Probably the most common belief concerning mirrors is that their breakage causes seven years of bad luck. Whatever the origins of this belief, here are some methods to counteract the curse.

• Throw salt over your shoulder.
• Directly after breaking the mirror, turn around three times counterclockwise.
• Burn the mirror, or at least blacken its shards in the flames of a fire. Save the fragments for a year and then bury them, and the curse will be counteracted (so you've only had to live through one year of bad luck).
• On the first night after breaking the mirror, light seven white candles and blow them out at midnight with one breath.
• Touch a tombstone with a piece of the mirror, and the hex will be lifted.

Any of these rites can be used, but bear in mind that the "curse" of the broken mirror is usually a self-created one.

Although viewed with suspicion by some, it is generally said that having a large number of mirrors in the home is lucky. This is probably because of the mirror's ability to deflect evil and attract good.

The mirror is symbolic of, among other things, money. Hang one beside the table in the dining room or kitchen to attract wealth and food to the home.

Ideally, no mirror should be hung so low that it "cuts off" the tallest household member's head (doing so may cause headaches). However, mirrors shouldn't be hung too high, either.

If you feel sorrowful or troubled while home alone, with no one to talk to and no apparent way out of your blue mood, stand before a mirror and gaze into your eyes. Your anxiety should disappear.

The idea that the positioning of your furniture affects your well-being and emotional stability may sound absurd, but think again. Most of us have rearranged furniture, even if only one or two pieces, until it felt "right." Our surroundings do influence our moods.

In magic, the shapes and positions of furnishings are just as important as other qualities, such as beauty, durability and value. In the magical household, furniture and other items should be arranged so that the energies of the house can flow unimpeded. To do otherwise is to live life less fully than is possible.

A harmonious household also allows positive outside energies—called *ch'i* by the Chinese—to enter the house in beneficial amounts, unimpeded, thereby lending energy.

Every home shapes its inhabitant's "luck" or life energies, no matter where it's located. But a home that serves as a refuge from the outside world is of particularly great importance in major metropolitan areas.

Most of us live in rectangular or square rooms and houses and are not aware that room corners are thought to be "traps" where positive energies can lie dormant. An easy remedy is to place furniture—such as chairs, screens or plant stands—in the corners, thereby cutting off right angles and allowing a smoother flow of energy throughout the room.

Furniture with rounded corners—no harsh, sharp edges—are ideal for the magical household. Round tables, curved chair backs and oval rugs allow luck and the house's energies to freely circulate, strengthening the house and its inhabitants.

A favorite chair facing your home's front entrance can symbolically guard the home. Even when you're not sitting in the chair, it represents your watchfulness over the home's well-being. In general, try to arrange your chairs so that they do not directly face one another; your guests will be more at ease this way.

To maintain a peaceful atmosphere in the living room, hang a painting or drawing of plants, such as evergreens, peonies or roses. The plants' symbolic presence brings their essence into the room.

Light, as important as furnishings in the home, symbolizes the Sun, Fire, wisdom, activity and growth. Though electric lights are commonly used to provide most of the light in a house, there are alternatives. Kerosene or oil lamps glowing softly in the house bring a spark of magic. They utilize Fire, the element of magical transformation, and their light is softer than that of harsh incandescent bulbs and fluorescent tubes.

Kerosene lamps are romantic and a perfect addition to the magical household. If you use one, follow the old tradition of submerging a small piece of red yarn or cloth in the oil. This guards the lamp against exploding and protects the family from death by poison or violence.

Candles, practically a requirement for magical workings, are also a pleasant touch when burned in the home anytime, day or night. Candles of specific colors can be used to lend their vibrations to the home.

White candles are generally burned during meditation and household purification rites, as well as to promote peace and spirituality. Green tapers lend healing energies, luck and prosperity to the home, while pink increases loving feelings and is ideal for entertaining, since it enhances friendships. Red candles lend protection and passion to those in your home, as well as magically shoring up the home's physical structure. Yellow candles promote calm, intellectual moods and are fine for study or reading.

Purple candles can be burned during times of illness or during household protection spells, since purple both speeds healing and is a source of extra power. Blue candles are burned in the bedroom at night for protection during sleep. They also induce prophetic dreams. Burn brown candles to solve any other home problems or to protect your pets. Beeswax candles, though expensive, are well worth the extra cost, since they spread a beautiful honey scent through your home.

Tiffany lamps and chandeliers, although quite costly, are magically potent and certainly far from ordinary. The stained glass of the Tiffany lamp charges the light from the lamp with color magic. By breaking up light, a good chandelier creates rainbows, increasing the house's flow of energy and lifting its vibratory rate. It refreshes the house.

Look at your home with an objective eye. Are its rooms pleasing? If not, take steps to improve the situation. You needn't spend a thousand dollars on new furniture. Instead, spend a few minutes thinking about and planning your ideal magical interior.

5   Dreaming

The bedroom is the temple of one of the most mysterious processes of human life: sleep. It also possesses two starkly contrasting sides. It is a nighttime world of blues and silvers and shadows, wrapping us in comfort and security as we drift off after a day of stress and pains. In the morning, however, the bedroom is bright and full of the promise of the dawn. In this room, we slip into the half of our daily selves that operates at its peak while we sleep. This "other self" is as real and important as our waking self.

Since even science hasn't yet been able to explain all of the secrets of sleep, and probably won't for some time, the old fears and ideas regarding this mystic process remain today: eating pickles before going to bed will cause nightmares; don't sleep with your head to the South; don't sleep in strange places. When the phenomenon of dreaming is considered, a whole new area of contemporary sleep magic is revealed. Many feel that dreams reveal much to the correct interpreter.

Sleep has been used in magic for centuries. Sleeping on a bull's hide at a crossroads revealed the future; high priestesses and priests in ancient times interpreted dreams for messages of the future or advice from the deities; and

31

Victorian girls cast spells to ensure dreams of their future husbands.

There are countless rites in which sleep or dreams play a prominent part, ranging from chanting a spell to cause drowsiness if sleep is slow in coming to taking control during a dream and manipulating it to accomplish magical goals.

Other factors are at work here, for many believe we travel in our sleep. When we close our eyes and still our minds, one of the most mysterious of human experiences—that of astral projection—may occur.

Of course, we do more in the bedroom than sleep. We read, watch television, talk and make love there, as well as slip into and out of clothing, think and daydream. Many involved in magic also set up ritual altars or work tables in the bedroom, adding yet another dimension to the room.

Although some of the topics discussed here—including dreams and astral projection—fall readily into this chapter, they can't be fully covered here. Check the Bibliography for titles of related books.

The ideal bedroom is large enough to move about in and is softly lit, with comfortable furnishings and a peaceful atmosphere.

Beds today are available in a wide variety of types. The standard sewn mattress and box spring are being challenged by water beds (said to induce prophetic dreaming and encourage love) and Japanese-style futons. Although synthetic fibers and all-cotton mattresses are the norm today, 100 years ago great attention was paid to the type of feathers used in the construction of the mattress.

For example, a mattress made of partridge feathers was thought to prevent disease in the sleeper, whereas one of pigeon feathers caused sleeplessness, until one's shoes were turned soles upward. Those stuffed with dove feathers were considered the unluckiest of all (especially for the doves).

Feather beds, in general, were thought to be effective protection against lightning, so many people lay on their beds during thunderstorms.

Before feathers were used, soft grasses and plants provided cushioning from the rough dirt or wood floor. This practice has survived in the form of herbal pillows, created for purposes ranging from promoting restful sleep to curing headaches.

No matter what type of bed you have, be sure it is parallel with the room's floorboards, if they are visible. This ensures that the energies that run through the house (traveling along the floorboards) won't encounter any obstruction lying crosswise.

The Chinese add that a beam or visible rafter in the ceiling over a bed will prevent sleep and may even cause sickness if the house's *ch'i* is so blocked directly above a helpless person. If you happen to have a beam over your bed, you can move your bed and rest easily. If this isn't possible or desirable (nothing is mandatory in magic), install a small mirror on the beam or the ceiling overhead to allow the energy to mystically escape through the mirror. You might get some strange looks, though, so consider the alternative: hang two hollow flutes or pieces of bamboo, each open at both ends, to the beam itself. This helps siphon away the excess power.

As you may know, there are certain traditional sleeping positions. The head pointing North increases stability, calmness, prosperity and quick recuperation from illness. Some say this is the ideal direction in which to sleep, for the North is a source of magical power.

The East has long been associated with religion and spirituality. It is also the point of intelligence, of sharp mental powers and freedom of mind. In this direction, the Sun and Moon rise, which has brought about the belief that one should sleep East to West, following the natural course of the heavenly bodies. Also, if you live in a hot area, sleeping with your head to the East might cool you down.

With your head pointing South during sleep, nothing but weariness and disease will afflict you, says old lore. This may also cause or aggravate insomnia. For those who are frequently sick, the simple act of moving the bed so that the head points North during sleep has seemed to produce miracles.

Sleeping with your head pointing West ensures love and spirituality, increases sensitivity of all kinds and promotes psychic abilities. It's ideal for those wishing to practice dream magic. It has also been used to promote creativity and so is recommended for artists.

Of course, you must be practical. If you can't move your bed to what seems like an ideal location, make do with what you have but place appropriate charms on the bed itself (those we'll discuss here) to offset any possible harmful effects from facing an undesirable direction (especially the South).

An all-purpose solution entails placing a small mirror somewhere on the bed facing the opposite direction: on the headboard facing South, for instance.

By the way, mattresses should be turned during the wane of the Moon, from the Full to the New. This will keep them flatter, since the Moon's powers of attraction are the weakest then.

The fortunate among us possess handmade quilts that grace our beds. Quilts are ideal blankets for the magical household, for the intricate patterns and loving attention devoted to their construction make them warm and safe things to wrap around us while we dream.

Quilts can have magical designs, especially if an industrious sewer decides to create one. Knot and interlacing patterns are considered fortunate, as are floral or herbal designs. Some think that quilts with square blocks or bright colors hinder sleep, while the "Rising Sun" pattern is said to be one of the luckiest of all.

There is magic in quilts. Tradition says they should be washed in melted snow to ensure that their deceased makers rest gently in the hereafter. And the first time you sleep under a new quilt or comforter, your dreams—good or bad—will come true.

Falling asleep, which should be an easy enough thing to do, confounds millions of us every night. For others, sleep may come, but it's far from restful to the body and psyche. There may be magical reasons if sleep comes hard only occasionally.

First off, mentally check your kitchen table and sink while you lay wide-eyed. Is the table clean? Did you wash the dishes? If not, you may have pinpointed the culprit, since dirty dishes prevent sleep.

If your table is clean, place a branch of leaves at the head of the bed. (It doesn't matter what kind, as long as the plant is not poisonous.) This is said to ensure restful sleep, as are lettuce leaves placed beneath the pillow, a lodestone tied to the headboard or post, or a piece of lapis lazuli worn to bed. Scattering salt between the mattresses or under the sheet also helps. One old charm is simple: When you wish to sleep, kiss your pillow and tell it so.

If these fail, stitch up a six-inch square pillow. Stuff it half-full with cotton batting, then fill it with celery seed. Sleep with this pillow on top of your regular pillow, if you use one; the scent should cause drowsiness.

Since our bodies are defenseless during sleep, it is important to safeguard them until our return to consciousness. Eucalyptus leaves or cinquefoil placed beneath the pillow guards our physical bodies, as does a knife under the bed—between the mattresses or lain on the floor.

A small mirror attached to the headboard will reflect any ill that may come near your sleeping body, as will a cyclamen or hoya (wax plant) grown in the bedroom. To protect the bed's contents, lay a broom beneath the bed. Anoint the posts with a protective essential oil, such as sandalwood, rose geranium, rosemary or frankincense. Then sprinkle a circle of salt around the bed (while inside the circle's perimeter), and you shall be guarded against all ill until morning. Sweep up the salt with the broom when you rise.

Sleep has been found to be an ideal time to heal the body of minor pains and illnesses, as well as to ward off future ills. A large red onion tied to a bedpost speeds recovery from any number of ills, including colds, and also protects the occupant(s) from future sickness, though you may get tired of smelling onions all night. If you try this, don't be surprised if you dream about Italian restaurants.

An old horseshoe stuck beneath the mattress helps relieve toothache pain, and a champagne or wine cork placed there may ease back pain. Any type of magnet, especially a horseshoe-shaped one, absorbs aches and pains when placed in the bed. Purists use lodestones (natural magnets) for this.

Fir branches hung over the bed guard against sickness or, if you're already ill, speed recovery.

Nightmares (the "mare" that brings bad dreams in the night) have long plagued us. Their origins are still open to speculation, but fortunately there are time-honored methods of ridding ourselves of these monstrosities.

A holed stone placed under the bed or tied to one of its posts, for instance, saves one from bad dreams, as does a knife or bit of steel slipped beneath the bed.

Purslane laid on the bed and vervain or mistletoe twigs hung on the headboard do their part in fighting off nightmares, as does a bit of wood betony or some silver under the pillow.

Eating balm before retiring was once a prescribed practice for ensuring a night of pleasant, relaxing dreams, as was sleeping on a small pillow of anise seeds or thyme.

Dreams seem to be of three basic types: psychic indicators of the present, future or past; half-recalled memories of astral projection; and wish-fulfillment and mental ramblings.

Most of us have had dreams that have "come true" or have worried when a dream repeats itself. Freud and Jung, a student of Freud's, did a tremendous amount of research on and work with dreams, making the age-old art of dream analysis once again respectable. They took dream interpretation out of a magical framework and nudged it closer to the realms of science.

Still, this hasn't lessened the impact or magic of dreams, nor has it explained why so many dreams do indeed materialize in people or incidents around us. Much more study needs to be done regarding dreams.

It's wise to keep a dream diary if you wish to work with dreams. Each morning upon waking, before rising from bed, write down everything you can recall of your preceding night's dreams in a notebook. Record the date, time you woke and any other factors that may have influenced your dreams, such as weather, emotional state or health.

If you have trouble remembering your dreams, try repeating this affirmation as you lie in bed before going to sleep: "I will remember my important dreams." If you do this each night, it should bear fruit.

When you read over your description of each dream, analyze it. What type of dream is it—psychic, memories of astral travel or wish fulfillment? (See the following descriptions.) Next, determine its importance. If it is a psychic-type dream, decide how best to act on it, but remember: We are not helpless instruments of Fate. We have the power to change our futures, for we are creating them every minute we exist.

Some dreams are psychic, because during sleep our conscious mind shuts down and the subconscious (or deep mind) is allowed to work free of restraint. This is our psychic, intuitive mind, which sends us images of possible future situations through the medium of dreams. It often does this symbolically, for the subconscious mind uses symbolism as a language. This must be remembered: A dream, even if psychically inspired, may not happen. Through symbolism, it may point to some other event or reality of your life.

A close look at such seemingly psychic dreams (as opposed to the other two types mentioned) can often reveal future trends or illuminate current conditions and attitudes we've unknowingly carried around with us. In other words, while psychic dreams don't always predict the future, they may provide revealing glimpses into secret parts of ourselves.

Astral projection is another matter entirely. This has been defined as the separation of the consciousness from the body. This isn't as strange an idea as it may seem, for there is a difference between the brain and the mind. The mind is nonphysical and, with the proper techniques, can be moved about at will.

There are many books that guide the student through exercises designed to facilitate astral projection, so I won't attempt to compete with them here. (See the Bibliography.) Though the concepts behind astral projection are quite simple, the phenomenon itself can be a harrowing, exhilarating and exciting experience. With practice, the consciousness, freed of physical bonds, can travel anywhere in the universe.

Most of us seem to astral project naturally early in life, before society thrusts down barriers of doubt and materialism. Few are able to enjoy complete freedom and ease of astral projection after youth.

We seem to project quite frequently but have no memory of the projections, as they are blocked by the conscious (materialistic) mind. Often, a dream seems so real that an occultist will say it happened "on the astral," i.e., that it had some basis in reality and was far different from a simple dream. Sometimes these "astral projections" are nothing more than wish-fulfillment. Some dreams may indeed be astral memories, and it is up to you to decide if they are and, if so, how you will let them affect you.

Whether such experiences are "real" in the material sense is not of consequence. They are effective, and anyone who has experienced and remembered such trips needs no validation.

The third class of dreams consists of those that are neither psychic nor memories of astral trips; they are mental ramblings. Think of them as visual doodling. The mind plays out the dreamer's fears and fantasies, scenes from famous movies or books, often with the dreamer center stage or playing a smaller role, watching. Too often, such dreams become wish-fulfillment: The movie star marries the wallflower who never goes out; diamonds and hundred-dollar bills flood out of pockets.

It takes practice and objectivity to separate such wish-fulfillment and doodling dreams from those that are truly psychic. It can be quite tempting to delude ourselves.

Psychic dreams can be created through magic. Before

going to sleep, empty your mind of all careless thoughts and narrow its focus. Concentrate on a question, if you have one. If not, simply relax, clean the slate and prepare for a night of psychic revelations (and a surprising morning).

Burning eyebright in the bedroom has long been done to cause psychic dreams, as has sleeping on a pillow of mugwort. The silvery-green herb is a potent dream-maker.

Sipping a glass of warm rosebud tea before bed may cause visions of the future in your dreams, but if you don't enjoy rose brew, try slipping an onion or a bay leaf under your pillow.

Additionally, heliotrope lain beneath your head allows you to see, in your dreams, a thief who has stolen your property. You may not see the crook's face, but symbols and clues from the dream can lead to the detection of the culprit.

Sleeping with moonlight flooding into your bedroom on the night of the Full Moon while wearing silver jewelry or moonstones creates psychic dreams, for the subconscious mind is ruled by the Moon, and so are dreams.

Find a small, sturdy mirror, preferably a round one. Ask a question as you place the mirror beneath your pillow at night. Just as the mirror reflects this world, so too does it reflect the future. Look for its message in your dreams.

If you have a question you wish answered in your dreams, write it on a piece of paper. Place nine rose petals on the paper, fold it three times and slip it under your pillow. Your dreams should reveal the answer.

On waking in the morning, try to make your first words pleasant, for this brings good fortune for the entire day.

If you are keeping a dream diary, don't look out the window first thing in the morning. To do so is to forget your dreams.

If you are plagued by constant nightmares and nothing seems to work, rise in the morning after experiencing one and describe the entire dream—to the Sun. You shouldn't be bothered again.

It isn't wise (in magical thought) to leave a bed empty for too long. Who knows what kinds of energies may settle there? So, if you must be away from home for some time and want to return home to a safe, clean bed, tuck a broom into it, laying the bristles on the pillow. If you have a broom reserved exclusively for magical practices, you can use it. Nothing will disturb a bed so guarded.

The bedroom is a place of romance, love and sex, and here again, magic can be utilized to make your dreams come true.

If you seek to find a love, light a wide red candle until it has a large reservoir of molten wax around its wick. Or, melt a small amount of red wax. When the wax is nearly cool but still malleable, place it on a glass or ceramic dish. Now take any three of the following dried herbs:

Rose	Basil
Dill	Ginger
Daisy	Thyme
Hibiscus	Vanilla
Licorice	Geranium
Rosemary	Juniper

Mix the herbs together in a small dish, concentrating on your need for love. Begin to knead the still slightly molten red wax, adding a pinch of the herbs every few seconds, until the wax is fully mixed with the herbs.

Form the wax into a small heart. Wrap it in pink cloth and suspend it from your bed.

If you wish to add zest to a decaying romance, sprinkle orris powder between the sheets, or add a few drops of patchouli or musk oil to the final rinse water when washing your sheets.

Before lovers or potential lovers come to visit, burn musk, patchouli, rosemary or vanilla incense in your bedroom to magically suggest your intentions and infuse the room with sexual vibrations.

Problems of sexual impotency can be alleviated by placing a piece of dried dragon's blood resin beneath the mattress or tying a branch from a fig tree to the bed.

To invite or increase love and sexuality in the bedroom, create a conducive atmosphere. Weave a spell by flooding the room with romantic or passionate thoughts.

Above all, love *yourself*—every morning when you rise, throughout each day and in the evening when you sleep. That's the greatest assurance of receiving love from others.

6   Stove and Spoon

Cooking is a magical process of transformation that utilizes the four elements: Earth (the food itself, which sprang from our planet), Fire (the source of heat—flame, solar, electric), Water (the liquid used to prepare or to cook the food) and Air (the steam that rises from the heated substance). Through the use of the elements, the cook prepares magically nourishing meals.

The earliest cooking, of course, utilized Fire. Vegetables and, less often, meat, were roasted on heat-hardened sticks. Liquids were warmed by dropping fire-heated rocks into leather or wood pots. There were no pantries; all foods could be obtained from the fields and forests.

When kitchens came into being, they were rarely idle. Soup-bubbling cauldrons hung over oak-scented fires in huge open-hearth fireplaces. Baskets overflowed with fruits, vegetables and scrubbed roots. Jars of herbs, flours, nuts, oils, honey and vinegar lined the shelves, awaiting future needs, and the air was heavy with the delicious scents of meals to come.

Today our fires and hearths have shrunk to metal boxes that plug into the wall. In much of the world, the cauldron has been left behind for skillets and crock-pots,

43

and the food processor has largely replaced the mortar and pestle.

Though our tools are modern, this doesn't lessen the culinary mysteries; the kitchen is still the altar upon which the cook's spells are wrought. Cooking is an act of magic in which the cook's manipulation transforms plain ingredients into something far greater than the sum of its parts.

In a sense, the cook is kin to the goddesses and gods who possessed magic cauldrons from which food flowed in miraculous quantities. Though the art of cooking today is often thought of as an unpleasant task, it can be an intriguing and wholly satisfying adventure, suffused with ancient ritual and tradition.

Because eating is necessary to life, so is cooking. We can pay someone to cook for us, or consume our meals in restaurants, but by doing so, we are missing the opportunity to truly become attuned to our food.

We are what we eat. Isn't it a comforting thought that, with magic, food becomes healthier, more readily used by the body? If we are to cook for ourselves, shouldn't we magically safeguard the room in which we prepare our meals?

This chapter isn't a guide to magical cooking; that must wait for a later date. However, it *is* a guide to the magical nature of the kitchen, its tools and processes. Even if your idea of cooking consists of gracefully shoving frozen dinners into the oven, the kitchen is still a place of magic.

There are many charms designed to safeguard the cook, the kitchen and the food prepared within it. One of the most pleasant ones directs us to grow an aloe vera plant in a sunny kitchen window. This plant has long been used to soothe burns and scrapes. To treat such an injury, gently cut off a mature, fleshy stalk, thanking the plant for its sacrifice, and squeeze the gel from inside the leaf onto the wounded area. The victim's pain will vanish as if by

magic, and, if the gel is applied conscientiously, the burn may heal almost overnight.

The aloe plant has magical properties as well. If grown in the kitchen, it guards the cook against food-preparation accidents that can be very nasty. When using aloe gel in the kitchen, dab some onto major appliances, windows, doors and tools to safeguard them, as well. If you can't grow the plant in the kitchen, it can be placed anywhere in the home.

Another popular kitchen protection is a rope of garlic, onions or peppers. These ropes can be purchased in gourmet shops and farmer's markets and are not only excellent protective devices, but they're also attractive. If you hang one of these ropes in the kitchen expressly for protective purposes, make sure it's never used for food, for the vegetables absorb negativity and spell danger to anyone who eats them.

A bulb of garlic placed on the kitchen window sill is also a fine magical ward, as is an onion. Leaded-glass crystal sun-catchers hung in a sunny kitchen window are also excellent protective devices.

Symbols such as pentagrams, equal-armed solar crosses and hearts can be painted, carved, chalked or traced with fingers or essential oils on canisters, cupboards, appliances, pots and pans—even dishes.

Some kitchen spells are designed to prevent hunger in the home. One involves filling a small jar with alfalfa and depositing it in the food cupboard. As long as it remains there, the family will never know hunger.

Another spell tells us to place pieces of sweet flag root (*Acorus calamus*) somewhere in the kitchen. Both this and the alfalfa guard against poverty.

A kitchen Witch bottle can be constructed to protect your food from contamination. Put three needles, three pins and three nails into a jar. Fill the jar with salt, seal it tightly, vigorously shake nine times and drip red candlewax over the seal. Then place it in the cupboard where it won't be seen.

Kitchen tools have magical natures. In the past, every kitchen contained a mortar and pestle. This was the definitive grinding and powdering tool, which has now been replaced by blenders, food processors and other grinding machines.

The mortar and pestle is rich with symbolism. The mortar, or cupped base, represents the female principle of creation, whereas the pestle symbolizes the male aspect. Together, they create change.

The mortar also resembles a cauldron, a sacred and magical tool. In fact, the mortar and pestle is so steeped in magic that a set placed in the kitchen (even if never actually used) will safeguard the room. They are so helpful, however, that it seems wasteful not to use them. A mortar is perfect for grinding spices, nuts and herbs for culinary and magical purposes. Practice using it until you grow comfortable.

When grinding, move the pestle clockwise within the mortar, otherwise you may unwittingly pour negative vibrations into the substance you're preparing. Also, keep your thoughts happy and healthy while grinding. If you wish, concentrate on the goodness of the food you're preparing or the magical virtues of the spices and herbs to be used as seasonings.

Since sets of mortar and pestles are fashioned of a variety of materials, many magical cooks collect them. For a set you plan to use, make sure to choose one with sturdy construction that is able to withstand heavy pounding. Glass and clay mortars break easily.

If you use a mortar and pestle for preparing herbs and nuts for cooking as well as for magic, keep separate sets so that a mortar in which holly and mistletoe have been ground won't be used to crush garlic.

Three other kitchen utensils—sieves, sifters and colanders—all have long magical histories. If hung or placed for protective purposes, they'll keep the kitchen secure. Some old sources say that to banish nightmares, place a sifter next to the bed while sleeping. The holes diffuse excess energies that might plague the subconscious mind.

Copper molds can be hung on the kitchen walls to lend their rich colors. Since copper is ruled by Venus, the planet of love, these molds bring love vibrations into the room.

Trivets have been used in the kitchen for centuries. Hot pots are placed on the three-legged metal devices (hence the name), which were often found beside the cooking fires of old.

Cast-iron trivets, which are fast becoming rarities, are worth collecting, for they are full of symbolism and magic. The symbols that commonly appear on trivets include brooms (symbols of domesticity, cleanliness and magical protection), hearts (representing love and protection), birds (creativity and freedom), flowers (passion) and pentagrams (protection).

The fact that trivets sit on three legs intimately connects them with magic, for three is not only one of the prime magical numbers, it is also dedicated to the Moon and the Goddess in Wiccan mysteries.

The stove, a tool of transformation dedicated to the element of Fire, was and sometimes is considered sacred. It should be kept clean, of course, though this can be the hardest magic to practice.

In China, some peoples believed that the stove should face southeast for best results. Because it was thought to harbor a god, such actions as weeping, cursing, singing, kissing and even chopping onions couldn't be done on or before the stove.

There are many kitchen spells that you can try. If you wish to perfect your execution of a recipe, copy it in red ink. Lay this on a flat surface in the kitchen. On top, place a red candle in a holder and light the candle. Let it burn down completely before you try the recipe. As it burns visualize yourself cooking the dish successfully.

When you burn food, cut yourself, drop pots and pans or experience a rash of accidents in your kitchen, a cleansing may be necessary. Get a shiny new copper tea kettle. Fill it with water (preferably bottled, spring or rain water) and add some bay leaves, rosemary, lemon peel (fresh, if possible) and cinnamon. Have a small quantity of salt as well. Place this on the stove, uncovered, and turn on the heat.

Next, place bowls or vases of fresh, colorful flowers throughout the kitchen while the water warms. As its scented steam fills the air, scatter salt evenly over the kitchen floor, then sweep it up and discard it outside your home. Place a whole onion beneath the kitchen sink to absorb negativity. (Replace it every month, if necessary.)

After a few minutes, turn the heat off. Allow the liquid in the kettle to cool, strain it through cheesecloth and sprinkle a few drops onto appliances, in the cupboards, in the sink, on the floor and so on. If you wish, add some to your mopping water and scrub the floor until it sparkles. Pour the rest of the water down the drain, and your kitchen should be fresh, cleansed and ready to do its magic once again.

A simpler cleansing consists of tying two dirty dishrags together in the middle, placing them in a pot of water with three bay leaves and boiling this for two minutes.

When the water cools, retrieve the rags and leaves and

pour the water down the drain or outside on bare earth. Bury the knotted rags outside with the leaves. Your troubles should disappear.

At one time, the fear of food being subjected to hexes and curses was rampant. For this reason, when food was being carried to the table it was covered to keep it spell-free.

It was once also widely believed that no food could be hexed if it had been salted, probably due to the magical and preserving qualities of salt. In fact, some old sources instruct us to throw salt into the food to blind the "hex."

Salt was so sacred in ancient times that the Romans revered Salus, the Goddess of Salt, Prosperity and Health. Roman soldiers were paid with salt, a practice echoed in our word "salary." Salt has played important roles in magic and religion from antiquity as a symbol of purity, life, eternity and wealth.

Speaking of salt, it is considered unfortunate to completely run out of the substance. This often forebodes loss of wealth, health or worse. To offset this, buy an extra box of salt and put it on a high shelf in the kitchen. You'll never use it, so you'll never run out of salt.

When cooking any type of food, from soup to zucchini, make the sign of the pentagram in the pan with a fork or knife. This guards the pan and the food, ensuring its wholesomeness. Chinese characters denoting health, wealth and prosperity are also traced in the pans.

The end product of kitchen work is, of course, consumed at meals. Eating is a mystical act, a joining of life forces that enable us to continue to exist.

In the magical household, what we eat is almost as important as how it is cooked. Many magicians today are strict vegetarians, while others eat a wide variety of foods, including meats. For a magical household to function properly, those residing in it should eat properly. A diet that includes fresh fruits and vegetables, whole-grain products, limited sugars and fats plus adequate (but not excessive) protein seems to be the healthiest way to eat today. Though some claim that an all-natural vegetarian diet is essential to magic, it isn't for everyone. In most cultures, meat is a secondary food source after vegetables and grains. The choice is yours.

Dining with others creates a unique bond. It is the basis for the ritual meals, such as communion, so common throughout religion. Once you've eaten with another person, you have established a link; even if you never see him or her again, you've shared this ritual.

Prayer before meals should be directed toward aligning with the food to be consumed, whether through recognition of a supreme being or a simple chant directed toward the food. This can also be done silently. Before eating, place your hands on either side of the food and send energy to the food through visualization. Receive its energy back and then enjoy.

The dining table is fraught with ritual. It should stand parallel to the walls so that the lines of energy running through the foundation will flow smoothly around it.

Since the dining table (and all tables) closely resembles an altar, such actions as sitting on the table or placing money or shoes there invite bad luck.

In setting the table, put the salt on first, and take it off last thing after the meal. The salt will guard the food and the diners. While dining with others, pass the salt with a smile.

Dishes of food are passed clockwise around the table to bless them with positive vibrations and ensure that they are healthy.

In earlier times, when poisoning was all the rage, many

rituals were carried out to prevent such calamities. If it was suspected that the food had been poisoned, a diner would jab a knife with a snake-bone handle into the dining table. The knife would quiver and shake if the food was tainted. Ivory chopsticks were once pushed into suspect food; if the food had been poisoned, the sticks would turn black.

Prior to eating any liquid with a spoon (such as soup or porridge), stir the bowl's contents from right to left (clockwise) three times, then withdraw the spoon and enjoy.

You might also wish to turn your beverage glass thrice sunwise before drinking to bless its contents. Whenever you make a toast, be sure that the glasses clink. If not, the toast won't be heard by the higher forces.

Always leave a morsel or two on your plate, for tradition says that they who clean their plates will know only poverty.

The first time you use a new set of silverware, make a wish. Visualize the wish every time you lift a fork or spoon and the wish may come true.

And if you're like many today who are trying to cut down on their food intake, whistle at the table. This can work to kill an appetite, though some consider it unlucky.

7   Bathing and Brushing

Until comparatively recent times, the bathroom didn't exist within the house. It has become so commonplace, however, that many of us have forgotten the days of pitcher and basin, the outhouse and the old claw-footed tub. True, the bathroom has become the site of such everyday acts as bathing, applying make-up and brushing hair, but a million spells are interwoven in the accomplishment of these tasks.

Today, bathing is an action that most of us take for granted, but the popularity of cleansing the body has gone through hard times. A powerful church, linking bathing with older Pagan religions, taught that cleanliness was kin to evil, causing Western Europe to suffer through centuries of abysmal body odors. Understandably, the popularity of colognes, pomanders, tussy-mussies, perfumes, pomades and scented clothing grew during this time.

Today we know the value of bathing. We no longer think of water as an enemy, and it's hard to imagine a time when swimming in the sea was considered injurious to one's health. The bath and its modern form—the shower—are here to stay.

Like most aspects of everyday life, bathing can be

viewed on many levels. While it may be nothing more than washing the body, a bath can also be a time to relax, forget worries, soak muscles, get friendly with a lover or perform magic.

The bath is a major part of magical ritual. Magicians and Witches are often instructed to ritually bathe prior to spells and rites. Contemporary Voodoo magic utilizes the bath as a means of attracting money and love, breaking curses, and blessing and protecting children. Innumerable spells involve bathing.

Why is the bath so popular in magic? Perhaps because it is a reunion with the element of water. Since our bodies are mostly water, and much of the surface of our planet is covered with this same liquid, we have a special affinity for water. Baptismal rites, which were part of many ancient religions, acknowledge this fact, as does the reverence for wells and springs found among many peoples.

In our hectic world, a quick shower is often substituted for a more leisurely bath. Many apartments lack tubs altogether, which is a shameful indictment of our busy lifestyles.Many prefer showers, but to indulge in truly magical living, baths are almost essential.

Baths can be effective in helping the ill to recover. The sickness can be magically transferred to the water and then sucked down the drain. (See *Earth Power** for details.) To purify the body, spirit and soul, simply add salt to a bath and soak for a few minutes. The salt neutralizes and eliminates negativity. Salt is also added to baths to aid in healing and to lend strength to the body.

There are many varieties of magical baths, each destined to offer unique benefits to the bather. Silver coins placed in a bath ensure money in the future, so this custom

---

* *Earth Power* by Scott Cunningham, Llewellyn Publications.

is often observed at a baby's first bath. A dip in goat's milk is said to help alleviate arthritis pains, while bathing in cow's milk magically increases one's beauty.

Collect some of the first snow of winter, melt it and add it to your bath. This will help keep you healthy throughout the year. Similarly, the first rain of May, if bathed in, will grant good health.

To cure a child, visit a cemetery between midnight and 1:00 a.m. Pull weeds from a grave (make sure they aren't poisonous), return home without looking over your shoulder and make a bath using the weeds. The child should be bathed in this water to aid in its recovery.

Bathing at various times and during certain seasons confers different magical blessings. In the morning, a bath increases beauty, as does washing the face with May dew. To take a dip at noon is lucky and fortunate, as it is during a Full Moon. Bathing at night may enhance psychic awareness. Some folks believe bathers should wash their hair every time they bathe or they might become ill.

A spell tells us to bathe on the Winter Solstice or the old Pagan holiday of Beltane (April 30 or May 1) with a penny wrapped in a washcloth. This ensures good fortune.

On Mondays, taking a bath just prior to sleep secures prophetic dreams. Tuesday baths increase passion, while Wednesday bathing strengthens the intellect. A dip on Thursday brings money your way. Friday baths help you find love (or increase the love you've found), while Saturday baths bring patience and thoughts of bygone days, perhaps memories of past lives. Those who bathe on Sunday will be stronger and healthier for doing so.

Baths can also be used in conjunction with magical rites. For instance, a spell performed on a Thursday to increase wealth could be preceded with a bath. (See *Magical Herbalism** for more on timing magic.)

Magical Herbalism by Scott Cunningham, Llewellyn Publications.

There are many plants, spices and fragrant oils that can be added to the bath for magical purposes. Lavender, rosemary and mint are among the most popular. Simply tie up the herbs in cheesecloth and drop the bundle in the tub.

The simplest nocturnal bath can be transformed into an exotic adventure with a minimum of preparation. Moonlight flooding in through open windows creates the proper atmosphere, as do white candles shimmering in the room. Oils and herbs added to the water, plus a bit of incense burning in the room, help set the mood. When all is ready, slip into the water, still your mind and let the moment overtake you. When you emerge, you will be refreshed and ready for meditation, recreation, sleep or a friend.

A bath spell. Fill the tub one-third full. Stand before it, looking down into the water. Through visualization, charge the liquid with a feeling, emotion or quality. For instance, visualize the water churning with dollar bills if you need money, or hearts for love. See the water infused with this essence, this power. Then slip into it and know that this energy is merging with yours.

You may wish to acknowledge the Full Moon with a Moon bath. Simply draw a half-tub of water, preferably cool but certainly not hot. Dip out about a quart of this water with a glass or crystal bowl. Then hold this outside for a few moments, letting the Moon's light flood the water. Then go back inside and add this water to your bath.

Add half a cup of milk, three drops of white wine and a bit of lemon peel to the water. Light a white candle and burn jasmine, lotus, gardenia or sandalwood incense. Bathe, feeling the Moon's cool, wet power flooding through you, nurturing and comforting you. If you wish, close your eyes and imagine the Moon directly above, shining in full glory.

After an appropriate time, dry your body and go about your activities. You have become attuned to the Moon and in doing so have strengthened yourself. Since the Moon is a powerhouse of magical energy, aligning yourself with it is a sound magical practice.

As you can see, bathing need not be mundane. It can and should be part of the wonderful daily experience of magical living.

Cosmetics were originally magical in nature. Make-up, a part of magical rites, was deemed necessary for the protection of the body. Cosmetics were also used for healing the sick, preventing evil from entering the body, warding off dangerous animals, increasing psychic powers and preventing the soul from escaping.

The eyes may have been the first part of the body thus guarded. Ancient Egyptians used kohl to outline and accentuate the eyes. The powder, expertly applied, formed a perfect oval through which the evil eye could not pass.

The Egyptians also painted their upper eyelids blue and lower lids green. This was thought to not only strengthen their optic powers but to provide protection. Most eye cosmetics were also originally intended to prevent blindness.

Lipstick had its origins in the colored fatty substances smeared on the lips to guard against the entrance of evil spirits or the exit of the wearer's soul through the breath. Coloring on the lips may also have been worn to prevent poisoned food from passing between them.

Finger- and toenails were painted or stained to guard these extremities. In some parts of the world, even today, permanent make-up applications are facilitated through the use of tattoos. Women in the United States have eyebrows tattooed on their faces. In the lore of sailors during the last 100 years, tattoos provide protection against drowning.

Eventually, such adornments were linked to beauty. In their earliest uses, however, cosmetics were considered magical in nature, used by women and men alike.

Cosmetic magic is not gone. Hindu women still smear black pigment on their eyelids to ward off evil. Women throughout the Middle East use henna to stain their hands and bodies with intricate designs, a practice that extends from at least ancient Egyptian times. This is done not only for beauty's sake but also to guard the woman.

The use of colognes, perfumes and scented oils spans the whole of recorded history. Such perfumed oils, originally used for religious and magical purposes, were poured onto images of deities or burned in oil lamps in their honor.

Since cosmetics and perfumes have their origins in magic, their use today can be infused with magical qualities.

Oils are frequently used in magic. If you need courage, dab on rose geranium oil. Feeling depleted? A drop of cinnamon or allspice oil should perk you up. If you're in the mood for love, try drenching yourself with tonka or rose oil.

Color is one of the most important aspects of cosmetic magic. Colors are powers, and through centuries of observation and use, each hue has acquired specific magical lore.

Cosmetics may be used in a truly magical rite to change your appearance. If you wish to carry a different face, stand before the mirror and concentrate on altering your face while applying make-up. This is a form of self-fascination that, with practice, can be mastered by anyone. When applying make-up, don't see *your* face in the mirror; visualize the one you wish to wear. Each time you look in the mirror, "see" your new visage. Others may notice your changed appearance but may not be able to explain it. Smile sweetly and keep your secret.

This technique can be used to improve your appearance, to diminish it (which has its advantages as well) or to completely alter your looks if you wish to avoid certain persons or move smoothly through a crowd.

Even for those women who don't wish to change their appearance, cosmetics can help in other ways. Applying lipstick with the firm knowledge that this ritual will help you more precisely express yourself is an excellent practice for women who speak before groups. The same can be done with any type of lip balm.

Eye shadow, liner or mascara can be applied with the intent of strengthening the vision. Fingernails should be painted with a specific need in mind so that the nails, and the hands to which they're attached, will reach out and grab that need.

If this seems silly, remember that these are rituals. Rituals provide us with easily understood, vivid demonstrations of our goals and needs. They are more than powerful psychological boosts, for they set energies in motion, which is the essence of magic.

Cosmetic magic is a personal practice, depending on your needs and desires. Just remember, while powdering and outlining, that there are magical rites thousands of years old behind your actions.

Here's a recipe for a woman's magical cosmetic that's easy to make: Take simple cold cream and place it in a crystal or glass dish or bowl. Add some rose water until the cream is scented. Blend until thoroughly mixed, then stir with a feather. If you anoint yourself with this magical cream, men will be attracted to you. Wearing it, you'll also be able to prevent quarrels with those you meet, according to old instructions.

Combing or brushing the hair is another daily activity loaded with magical overtones. There are thousands of spells and rites involving hair itself and for increasing or improving its appearance.

Some people are superstitious about hair. They feel that when hair is cut, magical powers decrease. Although hair is a manifestation of power, this is true of the entire body. Hair loss doesn't decrease our ability to perform effective magic, as ancient magicians and priests who ritually shaved their heads must have known.

Braiding or knotting the hair was once a common practice designed to foil negativity directed at the person. The knots or intertwinings spoiled baneful spells and also guarded the head. During protective rituals, women often tie up or braid their hair.

For centuries, red-tressed Witches were thought to be more powerful than blonde or brunette ones, and indeed, red hair figures into many old spells. This may be because of the color's solar associations.

When you brush or comb your hair, you can also brush in certain ideas or energies. If you wish to lose weight, for instance, stand or sit before a mirror, staring into your eyes, rhythmically brushing. Begin visualizing yourself happily turning down your favorite fattening foods, eating sensibly and wearing smaller clothing. If this spell is repeated daily and accompanied by increased exercise and decreased food intake, it can do wonders.

The comb was an early symbol of royalty. Used in magic to weed out evil, it also guards against the evil eye. Worshipers of Venus brought combs to Her shrines. A comb is placed on the altar during love spells.

If you wish to remain passionate, don't brush your hair after dark. This is a sure-fire way to lose your desire for sex. Then again, an old Persian spell instructs us to stand in the dark before a mirror, combing or brushing the hair without thinking, speaking or otherwise moving. Ghosts should appear in the glass.

There are some curious hair spells. To ensure fidelity, Gypsy lore says that the wife should take some of her own hair and bind it to some of her husband's. If she does this three times in full moonlight, while visualizing her husband happily staying at home, fidelity is ensured.

To promote heavy hair growth, a man should go to a brook or stream and, with his left hand, scoop up water against the current and pour this over his head.

If you fear losing your hair, an old Welsh folk spell may be just the thing. Simply rub your fingernails against each other for five or 10 minutes daily. How does it work? While rubbing, visualize yourself retaining a full head of hair as you mature.

Beards and mustaches are still looked upon with suspicion by many people. Some think they're evil while others believe that if a man combs his beard too often, it will increase his carnal desires.

There is also a curious belief that after washing the hair, you should eat and drink something before going to bed. If you don't, the fairies will steal you away while you sleep!

8 The Indoor Garden

If you love plants but don't have room for an outdoor garden, bring your garden indoors. Houseplants not only add life and vibrant green color to your home, they also bring some of nature's magic inside. When we coexist with plants, we grow closer to the forces of life itself.

House plants also lend specific influences or powers to their surroundings. You may wish to match plants with various rooms. For instance, plants that give off loving vibrations can be grown in the bedroom, protective plants near the front door, beauty and health plants in the bathroom and kitchen, and so on.

Some of the most popular house plants today, such as dumb cane (*Dieffenbachia*), are deadly poison and aren't recommended. These plants often emit strong vibrations that may wreak havoc in the magical house, disrupting its usually serene energies.

Following is a list of some popular house plants and their magical virtues. If you are diligent in caring for your plants, which depend on you for their survival, you can plant a mystic garden indoors, where you can appreciate its beauty and power in your daily life.

African violets are quite popular among many indoor gardeners who have no idea of their magical properties. Magically, under the influence of the planet Venus, these somewhat-difficult-to-grow plants promote spirituality and peaceful vibrations. Their five-petaled flowers are protective and link the plant with feminine divinity: the Goddess.

A lunar plant and member of the lily family, the ***aloe vera*** protects against intruders and accidents in the home, as well as negative energies. In Hawaii, the aloe is a good-luck plant.

The ***anthurium***, originally a South American plant, produces colorful, heart-shaped bracts (often mistermed "flowers") and glossy leaves. It is grown in large numbers in Hawaii and shipped to florist shops. Now more widely available on the mainland, this house plant lends love as well as beauty to the house.

The pit from an ***avocado***, when placed in water and allowed to sprout, will grow into a beautiful plant that will spread love throughout the house. Ruled by Venus, this plant may also increase sexual appetites.

The graceful ***bird's-nest fern*** offers protection to the home and its occupants, especially children and babies, and beauty to all.

Bromeliads bring luxury and abundance to the home, as well as exquisite beauty (especially the more exotic varieties). Magically ruled by the Sun, the plant has sharp points that deflect and defuse negative energies.

The ***cactus***, available in an incredible variety of species, is a protective plant that should be grown indoors (especially in sunny windows). If possible, have one cactus sitting in a northern window, another to the East, and so on. This helps safeguard the house against burglaries and intrusions. Also, cacti may be grown in the bedroom if you wish to cool your sexual urges. They are ruled by Mars.

The **crocus**, a Venusian plant that usually flowers in the spring, sends loving vibrations and peace through your home. Crocus bulbs can also be forced indoors for winter blooms.

Grown in the home, the **cyclamen** is protective, for no noxious spells can take effect where it lives. The cyclamen also guards against the effects of weather on the home. If grown in the bedroom, it protects you while you sleep.

All **ferns** are magically potent and have been used in occult protective practices for centuries. Any of the popular varieties can be grown in the home for this purpose, and they are especially effective if placed before large windows. Putting bits of tobacco in fern pots is said to increase their growth. The plant is ruled by Mercury.

Ivies of all kinds (ruled by Saturn) are protective as well as decorative, and never more so than when trained to grow outside on house walls. Potted and brought indoors, they serve the same function, for their curious stems and leaves drive all evil and negativity from their dwelling place.

Orchids usually bring love to mind, though in the Orient they are thought to induce chastity! Either way, they make great house plants for those with the patience to tend them. They are governed by Venus.

Palms, solar plants, are also spiritual. Where grown, they emanate uplifting vibrations. Their high spiritual qualities caused them to be linked with religious and magical practices in early times.

The **Norfolk Island pine** grants protection against hunger and evil if grown in the home. It is a perfect tree for use at Yule, and its very shape reflects its magical potency.

Considered very lucky and rare, the **San Pedro cactus** possesses curative properties. It is associated with the four winds and is quite a protective plant, playing a major role in Mesoamerican religious and magical rites.

Love and abundance-bringers, **succulents** can be among the easiest of house plants to grow. Choose ones that appeal to your mystic sense. Succulents are ruled by the Moon.

The *ti* (or *ki*) plant, popular in Hawaii as well as on the mainland, is an all-around good-luck plant with a wealth of magical uses. In Hawaii, it is still utilized in magic, often being placed on altars or used to wrap offerings left at ancient stone *heiau*, or temples. Grown in the home, the ti is protective and draws positive vibrations. The green variety is best and was the only one known to ancient Hawaiians. The red ti, supposedly a carrier of ill luck, is dedicated to Pele, who, as a volcano goddess, is associated with destruction as much as with creation. According to contemporary mainland folk magic, the ti grown in the home will attract money if a coin is placed beneath it. The plant is ruled by Jupiter.

Tulips are good safeguards against poverty and desperation. Ruled by Venus, it is also a plant of love. If you are given a tulip in the spring, grow it carefully. Save the bulb and replant it the next year for more love and money.

The **Venus's-flytrap** may seem to be a strange house plant, but these fascinating, insect-eating plants are readily available at many nurseries. Though dedicated to the goddess of love, they are usually brought into the home for their protective qualities. They can also be grown specifically to "catch" or "trap" something, such as luck, money or a job.

Some say the **wandering Jew** is unlucky to grow in the home, but I don't know anyone who can confirm this. The plant's leaf structure betrays its protective qualities. The wandering Jew is ruled by Mercury.

The **wax plant**, with its stiff, wax-like leaves and star-shaped flowers, is popular among magicians because of its resemblance to the pentagram. Ruled by Saturn, it is grown indoors to confer a net of safety around the home.

The *weeping fig*, though somewhat difficult to grow, will confer restful sleep if placed in the bedroom. In the kitchen, it guards against poverty and hunger. Anywhere else in the house, the weeping fig provides good luck and prosperity of every kind.

9 Fur, Fins and Feathers

There has always been a natural kinship between animals and practitioners of the magical arts. Many animals have become intimately woven into religious and magical systems and been revered as gods or damned as devils.

In earlier times, the familiar or magical pet was the mediator between the Witch or magician and the forces of nature. Through cohabitation and ritual, the Witch and familiar formed an unusual bond that was often utilized in magic.

Millions of people with no interest in the occult arts have formed satisfying relationships with animals, too. Psychologists even tell us that pets can help us maintain good mental health.

While humans are in many ways civilized, animals are not. Their hearts beat with the rising and setting of the Sun, the excitement of the chase, the comfort of the pool, nest, burrow, branch or hollow. Animals are closer to the Earth and its powers; they hear the music of the universe to which many of us have closed our ears.

Like animals, those adept in magic live in harmony with the pulses and rhythms of nature. To change any part of the universe, we must be attuned to it. Developing loving

69

relationships with animals is a fine start.

When we invite animal friends to share our homes, or leave them food and water outside to let them enjoy their freedom, we create psychic bonds between human and animal. This forms a direct link with the Earth and its powers.

Many words could be written concerning this mystical rapport. Animal lovers report the development of forms of inter-species communication that actually work. Psychic messages from pets seem to be received from time to time. Pets lost or inadvertently left behind during a move often appear at the door of the new residence, hundreds or even thousands of miles away.

All types of pets can be a boon to the magical household. Their movements may foretell future events or weather patterns. Cats, dogs and birds (among others) possess keen senses, both physical and psychical, and can be taught to guard the home as psychic watchers. They often notice the approach of strangers long before our senses signal their presence.

Since animals are important household members, they should be mystically guarded. There are a variety of charms for protecting them against accidents, disease and theft. The following examples can be adapted for use with most types of pets.

Buy a small bell of any type. It should have an audible ring. Suspend this from the pet's collar, visualizing the ring guarding the pet. The ringing bell will automatically banish negativity as the pet moves. A bell can also be hung from the pet's cage or placed in its bed.

On the back of a pet's tags and licenses, you can mark protective symbols and signs, such as pentagrams. You can also make a round, metal tag of your own, scratch or carve mystic words or symbols on it and hang it with your pet's

other tags.

For animals that must reside within cages or tanks, such as fish, some birds, reptiles and insects, attach some protective object to their home. Holed stones, quartz crystals, seashells or even tiny pieces of paper on which you've inscribed a spell of protection that you wrote yourself work well. Or, encircle the cage with pure white wool yarn or a cord that contains nine knots.

A necklace of shells protects animals from the adverse effects of the evil eye and also helps them love you. You might attach a small, rounded shell to the animal's collar.

There are also spells to ensure that your pets won't leave home. While this should be the animal's decision, we don't want them to leave before they've gotten to know us. These charms may make the difference.

Hold up your pet before a mirror. If it seems to notice its reflection, it will remain at home. Or, if you have a fireplace, have the animal look up the chimney. Such spells are best performed on the day the animal arrives.

An age-old practice of attuning an animal to your vibrations consists of allowing it to eat from your plate when you've finished a meal. The few morsels the pet consumes will strengthen its relationship with you.

Certain spells are specifically designed to remind a cat to return home after its nocturnal wanderings. First, attune yourself to the pet; stroke or cuddle it, or simply gaze at it. Align your breathing. Visualize as you do any of the following spells.

Putting a small dab of sugar in a cat's mouth on a Friday morning at 9:00 is said to be quite effective. Then again, there's the old standby of buttering its paws. If a cat does indeed run away but is recovered, hold it and gently swing the animal thrice through the air. This will attach it to the house.

A dog may be kept from straying by placing a few

hairs from its tail under the steps of the house's entrance. Another curious rite involves putting a piece of cheese in your boot heel!

The most effective spell for ensuring that your pets stay close to home is composed of three ingredients: proper feeding, adequate attention and love. These will weave a magical spell that is powerful enough to guarantee your pet's continued presence.

In earlier times, when pets acted strangely, they were thought to have fallen victim to evil spells. Thus, counterspells evolved to break such charms and release the helpless creatures.

Today we're a little wiser; we know there aren't black magicians hiding behind every wall hexing our pets. But when they seem listless or out of sorts and no medical problem has been diagnosed, you may want to try some of the following rites—just in case!

The easiest spell consists of sprinkling salt in an unbroken circle (going counterclockwise) around the creature. If you can do this before the pet moves from the circle, it should be cured. (Sprinkle salt around the cage if the animal lives in one.)

Feeding your pet the core of a quince is also said to cure bewitchment. If you can't find any quinces, or if your pet won't eat one, try to get the animal to walk (fly, swim, slither or crawl) in a counterclockwise circle three times. If this can be accomplished, the spell will be lifted.

Another major concern with pets today is thievery. Here are three spells designed to guard your pets from stealing hands.

According to old instructions, go into your backyard at sunrise, have the pet sit quietly and, naked (how private is your backyard?), run thrice around the pet, saying at every turn:

> Thief, your eyes shall never shine
> On this animal of mine!
> Thief, your hands shall never find
> This guarded animal of mine!

Or, take the animal to be protected to a crossroads at midnight. Let a few hairs (feathers, etc.) fall from the animal to the ground and say:

> Crossroads,
> Pathways, attend to me:
> This beast shall not be pulled on thee!

Finally, take a few hairs, feathers or some other part of the animal (or, failing this, draw as exact a likeness of the creature as your talent allows). Place this, with protective herbs (such as juniper, basil, bay, rosemary, dill, vervain, St John's wort, etc.), into a small box. Seal the box and tie it shut with nine white cords. Bury it on your property, as close to the house as possible. Your pet should be safe from thieves.

Animals have long been recognized as possessing special powers, that are often used in magic. This has sometimes degenerated to the point that the animal was killed for a part of its physical form (the lucky rabbit's foot, for instance). Obviously, it is more humane to invite the animal to live with us, so that it naturally bestows its powers on our lives and household simply by its presence.

Here's a look at some of the symbolism and magical influences of a few common and uncommon pets. If some of these "pets" seem strange, remember that magicians respect and love all creatures, even those that we have been taught are "evil," disgusting or dangerous.

Bat

The bat, long associated with the mysterious, is sometimes kept as a pet. It is thought to confer long life, happiness and wealth to those humans with whom it lives. Sacred to Persephone and ruled by the planet Saturn, the bat is sometimes considered to be the luckiest of all animals.

Bird

The phrase "a little bird told me" harkens back to the time when birds were watched to divine the future. Long revered for their ability to fly, these winged creatures are great companions.

If you wish to try a type of bird divination, approach your bird, just before sunrise and in strict silence, with some of its favorite seed in your hand. Ask a question that can be answered positively or negatively, or simply meditate upon your future. Then throw some seed to the bird or fill its bowl. If the bird eats, the signs of the future are favorable, or the answer is yes. If not, the reverse is true.

Birds in the home can increase the memory and mental powers of those humans residing there. They are lively companions, ruled by Mercury. Their fallen feathers can be kept and used in spells.

A gray feather attached to a package sends good fortune to your friend, while a blue one ensures health and green increases money. Tying several feathers together and hanging them over the bed prevents nightmares. Feathers are also used in travel spells due to the bird's ability to fly. A little wreath made of feathers placed beneath a sick person's pillow will help speed recovery if the wreath was fashioned while the craftsperson visualized the patient as healthy and fit.

Feathers were also once placed in doorways, with the mystic intent of halting wandering children from passing through, and burned beneath the bed during a difficult childbirth to ease the process.

Every bird possesses a distinct personality, as do all animals. Generally, birds are energetic and affectionate. But be warned: Though birds are great housemates, stuffed birds, pictures of winged creatures or wings of any kind in the house are considered taboo. Such objects are said to block the proper flow of energies through the house, thus causing it to lose its luck.

Even feathers can be suspect; many people will not have a peacock plume in the home. The best feathers to use in magic are those that have either fallen naturally to the ground or been collected from pets after they have lost them.

Canary

The canary, due to its bright yellow color, is sacred to the Sun. It has long been kept in the home for its fine song, its legendary ability to promote harmony and happiness in the home and its assurance of good fortune. To ensure safe hatching of its eggs, place a sage leaf among them. For the best possible fortune in a house, keep both a canary and a goldfish (think of their colors).

Cat

The cat, long revered and feared, is by its nature a mysterious creature. Its independence and nocturnal habits have earned it a large place in folklore and magic, linking it to innumerable myths, legends, rites and spells.

The cat's nighttime activities and large, glowing eyes firmly connect it with the Moon. It was sacred to Bast, Freya, Isis, Sekhmet, Astarte and Diana, among other deities, and is forever associated with the Witch and magic throughout Europe.

In Britain, the black cat is generally looked upon as bestowing favorable vibrations, whereas in the United

States it is viewed with caution, as a negative influence. To ensure good vision and alleviate any irritation of the eyes, stroke a black cat's tail (unless allergies prohibit this).

Watching a cat can reveal much of the future, according to ancient lore. If, while lying down, a cat turns its tail toward the North or East, a storm may be headed your way; if it turns to the South or West, the weather will be calm and clear.

When a cat washes her face, expect a visitor to arrive shortly. After the cat has washed, the direction to which it first looks is that from which the visitor will arrive.

There is a large body of such lore, obviously evolved from observations of cats and their habits. Watching a cat go about its daily business can be an enjoyable form of divination and is ideal for cat-lovers.

A cat of three colors is extremely lucky and will keep a house from harm, while a smutty-nosed cat will bring wealth to its companions. Orange or tabby cats were once thought to be specially favored by Witches.

Stroking a cat's tail nine times grants good luck at cards, so if you're planning to play bridge or poker, give the cat some extra attention first; no one need know what you're doing!

One charming story concerning cats and their mystic powers relates that a woman who mistreated her cats consistently suffered rainy washdays. (This was during the time before electric and gas clothes dryers, when all laundry was dried outside.) Thus, by some sort of psychic retaliation by the cats, the woman's wash never dried properly.

Sharing your home with a cat will bring it many blessings, and working with cats is one of the most rewarding forms of all animal magic.

Chameleon

The chameleon, with its ability to change its colors to

match its surroundings, is an ideal pet for those who don't wish to be noticed. The chameleon is ruled by the Moon because both are changeable but neither really changes.

Anciently, it was believed that the chameleon guarded against the evil eye. Today the animal has a reputation for warding off disease and increasing sexual appetites if kept in the bedroom, and is also believed to make humans more adaptable.

Cricket

Popular pets in the Orient, crickets are often placed in metal cages and kept on the hearth. They are said to promote mirth and plenty.

A cricket can be kept in the bedroom as a watchdog. Normally, the cricket chirps all night. Since the chirping stops only when a stranger enters your home, silence will awaken the household.

Dog

Dogs have been well loved as pets and have found their place in many magical and religious rites. The ancient Egyptians, Babylonians, Assyrians and others revered the dog.

This creature is ruled by Venus, the planet of love (though some say the Moon is actually in symbolic charge). As such, the dog increases the love in any home in which it lives.

However, dogs are also under the dominion of Hecate, the Greek goddess of dark forces. It was thought that of all creatures, including humans, only dogs could see this goddess. They warned of her approach with howls and barks. Sensitive to the unseen, dogs are frightened by ghosts and specters but will alert you to such dangers. If you have trouble with your dog howling at night (and it isn't signaling danger), turning your shoes upside down is said to quiet it.

Sacred to Diana, Hecate, Anubis and other gods and goddesses, dogs are excellent watchers and extremely loyal to their home turf. They are sometimes called upon to spread protective energy around the home.

If you share a pillow with a dog, you'll also share your dreams. (And possibly fleas.)

Fish

Fish are pleasant, watery creatures that bring love and blessings to any home. If you wish to entrance yourself naturally, watch a fish slowly swim in circles until you feel your everyday consciousness begin to shift.

Goldfish are kept in aquariums to attract money to the household (due to their gold color), to ensure fertility if this is a problem, to strengthen marriage or relationship bonds or even to offset negative energies, since they are magically ruled by the Sun.

Frog

The frog, long associated with magic and the occult, was an early symbol of inspiration. In earlier times, it was dedicated to Ptah, Venus, Heket and Hecate and was kept as a pet, perhaps in the garden, to increase its fertility.

A frog may be kept in the home or outside to attract new friends and acquaintances, if you'd like more company.

If a frog casually hops into your home, see it as the omen of good luck that it is said to be and hope that it decides to go (leaving the luck behind). Woe be to him or her that kills a frog. Severe bad luck results.

If rain is needed, try taking the garden frog inside the house and placing it, for a few moments, in a dark spot. This invokes the rain god to send showers.

The frog is also a symbol of resurrection and is ruled

by the element of Water.

Iguana
The iguana, ruled by the planet Mars, is said to increase bravery in anyone who adopts one into his or her life. A strange, dinosaur-like creature, the iguana is great fun to watch walk or quietly munch lettuce. Unfortunately, they don't have much of a consciousness humans can reach.

Lizard
Lizards in general are ruled by Mars and help keep disease from the home. They are also protective.

Monkey
The monkey, ruled by Mercury, is sacred in many parts of the world to this day. Its presence in the house ensures health, success and good fortune.

Newt
Who hasn't heard of "eye of newt and toe of frog"? Newts can be great pets. Ruled by Venus, they bring love if kept in the home and attuned to.

Owl
Like newts, owls generally require live food. If this offends you, don't think of keeping an owl. Long famed for their wisdom and feared as a death omen, owls impart intelligence and watchfulness to their housemates. They are sacred to Athena and are ruled by Saturn.

Parrot
The parrot is said to improve the wit of all that live with it. It is certainly a fascinating creature and can be endlessly entertaining.

When a parrot whistles, close the windows—rain will be arriving shortly. Teaching a parrot to say sacred names or lucky words will bring the best of luck to both you and the bird.

Snake

The snake is an ancient symbol of wisdom, eternity and reincarnation. Traditionally, a snake kept in the house brings it good luck. In parts of ancient Egypt, the snake was revered as the guardian of the home, lending good health to its inhabitants.

In ancient Crete, milk to drink and low tables were provided to household snakes by homeowners who thought their presence blessed the home.

The snake represents longevity, eternity, wisdom, reincarnation, health and virility. Today, it is gaining in popularity as a pet. For centuries, it was sacred to Aesculapius, Mercury, Quetzalcoatl, Wadjet and others. It is ruled by Mars.

Spider

The spider can be kept in the home as a pet but is more often found roaming around in its territory. Never kill a spider; it's mean and unnecessary.

The spider is known for its dexterity, spinning and weaving skills and determination. Therefore, if you are a spinner or weaver, this is an excellent pet.

The Chinese consider the spider to be protective, while others maintain that it increases intelligence.

Spiders are associated with Spider Grandmother, a creatress goddess of the Navaho tradition, and Arachne, a fabulous weaver who was transformed into a spider in Greek mythology. Witches often stare into spider webs, which are objects of contemplation and meditation, and some magicians use webs like crystal balls to scry the future.

Toad

Toads were once more popular pets than dogs or cats. They are reputed to increase intelligence and are protective of the area in which they live. Ruled by Saturn, toads are sensitive and react to ghosts and psychic energy.

Some toads secrete a poisonous substance called butotenin from their skins. This has been shown to contain hallucinogens, but it won't cause warts.

Toads should definitely be kept outside. Keeping a toad in the cellar or anywhere inside the house is not recommended.

Turtle

The turtle, ruled by Venus, is a symbol of longevity and fertility, especially for women. It also is said to ensure health. Turtles are such strange creatures that magicians have kept them as pets through the ages. If you want to change your luck from bad to good, simply pat a turtle's shell.

During a thick fog, a turtle can be taken out of its water and placed on the ground to clear up the mists.

Turtles will bring luck to the house.

According to ancient lore, an uneven number of pets in the home is favorable, while an even number is unfavorable. Keep this in mind when deciding who—or what—will come to live with you next.

10   The Mystic Garden

For those of us blessed with land attached to our homes, a mystic garden is an excellent addition to the magical household. A garden brings beauty and ensures a steady supply of fresh and dried herbs. It also spreads an aura of protection around your home, shielding it from the outside world. When people approach, even before they've stepped over the threshold, they will have been enchanted by the garden's subtle powers.

Not everyone has the space to plant a garden, but even apartment dwellers can grow herbs and flowers on window sills or porches in pots and planters. Indeed, a garden can be maintained indoors with house plants. (See Chapter 8.)

Still, an outdoor garden is worth creating if you have the time, space and inclination. In fact, it is an ideal setting in which to perform magic. Spells cast in gardens are more powerful than those done indoors, for the forces of nature resident in the plants around you and the solid earth beneath your bare feet align with your own powers to produce the needed results.

Magical Herbalism describes one method of creating a magic garden. There are countless others—in fact, you should let your imagination run wild when fashioning your mystic green corner.

A magic garden need not advertise its powers. It can be your secret with the Earth. Since no one seems to think twice about herbs or fruit trees growing in a garden, on the stairs or in window boxes, why not pick plants that will bring wealth, protection and love to your home?

Your garden can also be a source of help in fulfilling your personal magical goals. If you wish to improve your psychic powers, for instance, plant a *bay tree, common celery, honeysuckle, marigolds, roses* or *thyme*. While thriving in the garden, the plants will help attune your home to psychic vibrations. Plus, their flowers, leaves and seeds can be used in magic rites to further accentuate their effects.

Those desiring a loving household may wish to include such common plants and flowers as the *gardenia, primrose, spearmint, tomato, pansy, jasmine* and *catnip,* and (if space is no problem) a few trees, such as *cherry, apple, orange, maple* and *willow.*

To ensure happiness in a home, you might wish to fill a window box or ranks of flowerpots with *hyacinth, lavender, marjoram, catnip* and *morning glory* (careful—it creeps everywhere).

If money is a problem, you could choose *mint, onion, snapdragon, camellia, chamomile, clover, dill, basil* and perhaps even a small section of *wheat. Pine, oak, ash* and *apple* trees planted near the house also help direct prosperity your way, as will a *banana* plant.

To ward off thefts in your home, plant a "fence" of *ti (ki)* around its perimeter, or be sure to include *garlic, cumin, vetivert,* a clump of *thistles,* an *aspen, cactus* or a *juniper* tree.

Bamboo and *hydrangea* near the home offer it general luck, as does a *sunflower,* which is sometimes con-

sidered a prerequisite for a garden in Mexico. *Myrtle*-filled window boxes, if planted by a woman, are lucky too. A *bay* or *palm* tree in the garden protects it and your home against inclement weather.

When all is growing greenly, no one will be the wiser concerning your garden's powers, although every plant is virtually a spell in and of itself.

Choosing your flowers, trees, herbs and vegetables with their powers in mind brings a new dimension to gardening that truly makes it a part of magical living.

Many magical gardeners place an altar in their gardens, at which they burn incense in honor of the ancient vegetative deities: Pomona, Faunus, Bacchus, Priapus, Demeter, Pan, Tammuz, Dionysus, Isis, Adonis and Enkimdu. These and many other goddesses and gods are intimately connected with the Earth, vegetation and horticulture, and all can be called upon to watch the garden and lend it fruitfulness.

A garden altar can consist of a statue (or other image of a particular deity), a composite figure or no image at all. A small, roughly rectangular rock may be placed on the ground to stand upright like a pillar and a flat, rounded rock laid before it to serve as the offering stone. Bits of grain, gemstones, money, milk, water or wine can be placed on this stone in honor of the nature gods of old. The garden shrines to Bacchus were nothing more than old stumps erected in his honor.

If these two rocks are placed in an inconspicuous location, they will attract little attention from wandering eyes and will seem to be a part of the garden itself (which they undoubtedly are).

If you decide that even a primitive altar is not for you, simply think of the entire garden as a place of homage to the vegetative deities.

Incense can be burned in your garden at regular intervals. Stick incense works perfectly and can be conveniently pushed into the ground.

You can also burn incense in conjunction with planting a new addition to your garden. For instance, Dave burned incense the night he planted his first rose bushes. At night, under the Moon, tread your garden's perimeter a mystic three times, holding smoking incense, visualizing your garden as healthy and flourishing. Again, use your imagination.

Small images of animals can be placed in the garden as well; deer, ducks and the like are readily available. Each animal is associated with ancient deities and rituals, who call upon the animals represented to help bless and protect the garden.

If you wish to include a statue or other image in your garden but don't feel comfortable honoring old gods, you may place a "garden guardian" there to protect your garden from negativity.

Take an image, statue or stone, and, standing in your garden, lift the image ceremonially to the four directions. Begin in the East and move to the South and West, finally ending in the North.

Next, pour red wine or apple cider over the stone to empower it with life. Charge it with your powers of visualization to magically guard the garden and house and all that dwells within them. Place the guardian in a focal spot in the garden.

There are other garden-protection spells. The simplest is to trace the following sign in the earth with your finger or the blade of a magical knife. (If you don't have a magical knife, it doesn't matter, for your finger is the original magical blade.)

$$+ \ \heartsuit \ +$$

Creating this symbol aligns the garden with your intentions and home, guards it against negative energies and even protects it from the doings of mischievous fairies! Repeat this simple ritual every three weeks or so.

Another method entails marking the following sign on the garden wall or walkway with a piece of plaster or chalk:

To guard trees, bury horseshoes beneath their roots. Plants may be protected by drawing circles in the earth around them, or by loosely tying small bits of brightly colored cloth to their stems. One of the most effective methods is the construction of a knot garden, in which the hedges and paths are laid out to create endless, interwoven knots. Maze gardens are equally protective of both plants and the adjacent home.

Some people place a huge Witch ball or gazing globe in the garden. The gazing globe is a glass sphere silvered on the inside and usually placed on a stand. Not only does it reflect evil and absorb the powers of the Sun, Moon and stars, but it is also beautiful; the entire garden and sky are reflected in its surface.

If you wish, try sitting in the garden on a quiet day, gazing at the Witch ball with your eyes half-closed. Relax and look at (and *into*) the sphere; let your conscious mind drowse and allow a glimpse of the future.

If you have an old-fashioned well or spring in your garden, it will add its own powers, for wells have long been symbols of the feminine powers of nature. Since water is intimately connected with wealth and money, a well may bring prosperity to the home. It can, of course, be used for wishing magic.

You might also want to make a Witch's wheel of fortune. Step out nine magic paces from the well and set up an old wooden wheel. Train morning glories to grow on, over and through the wheel. This will guard your property and ensure that all who live in both home and garden do so in harmony.

A crescent-shaped pool circling away from the house will grant it prosperity and love, and is quite popular in China and the East.

In gardening, insects are always a problem. Though there are hundreds of pesticides on the market, more and more farmers and gardeners are turning to organic methods, avoiding the use of hazardous chemicals that poison our environment.

In the old days, before pesticides were available, gardeners and farmers had other methods of routing unwanted garden visitors.

One of the most ancient, dating from classical Greece, consists of writing a short note to the pests in question (slugs, snails, aphids, mice, etc.). The message should be politely worded and ask the offending creatures to leave the garden quickly and forever. The note should also contain a warning that if they don't leave, retribution in the form of poisons may be used. The note is well-greased and left on an unhewn stone in the garden at dusk. The creatures, in theory, will read the message, eat it and depart, never to return. (We can't guarantee this spell's effectiveness.)

It would be more practical to buy ladybugs or praying mantis from your nursery and release them in the garden. They'll happily live off aphids and other plant-eating insects. The ladybug was sacred to the Norse Goddess of

Love, Freya. To see a ladybug is lucky; to purposely kill one quite the reverse.

Magic, the position of the stars and the phases of the Moon have long ruled gardening practices.* Weeds, for example, should be pulled in the wane of the Moon, before Midsummer, for the most effective eradication. But remember: Weeds can be good friends; they're just herbs with different names.

Transplanting has its own rules. A tree can be transplanted at any time of the year, during the waxing Moon, as long as you water it every day, exactly at noon, and continue this faithfully until the first rains.

According to old instructions, transplanted trees must be placed in a position relative to their former position— e.g., the East side of the tree should still face East in its new home.

If you plant a lawn, mow it during the Moon's first and second quarters for lush growth or during the Moon's wane for a decrease in growth.

There are some peculiar garden spells. To stop ghosts from walking through your green corner, boil prickly-pear roots in stump water, then sprinkle the yard with the mixture. If you're fresh out of stump water, lilies planted in the garden will do the same job.

If you have an ash tree near the house, you might try the following rite: On a Sunday at dawn, hang a wreath of flowers on the tree, and the household will be guarded against snakebite for the rest of the year.

Most plants, especially food crops, are steeped in planting ritual. Much of this is astrological in nature. Beans, for example, must be sown on the Full Moon or a few days after. Cabbage should be the first plant cultivated in the

---

* See Llewellyn's Moon Sign Book for complete instructions and dates.

garden of a newly married couple, for this ensures good fortune in their gardening and relationship.

Cucumber seeds are best sown in the first lunar phase, the New Moon, when the Moon is in Cancer, Scorpio or Pisces. It was once thought that for best results, they had to be planted by a young naked man. To protect cucumber plants from insects, plant them on May 1 (the old Pagan holiday of Beltane) before sunup.

If you consider yourself intelligent, don't try growing gourds. According to ancient lore, you must be a bit dense to grow good gourds.

Lettuce, on the other hand, thrives for the smart as well as the ignorant if planted on St. Patrick's Day. Too many lettuce plants in the garden may cause sterility, however.

Onions are planted during the waning Moon, since they are an underground crop. To double your yield of onions, plant them upside down using your big toe.

Potatoes, sown during the Moon's third quarter, are also bound by harvest magic. When they are dug up, all household members should taste them, otherwise they will rot. By the way, potatoes shouldn't be planted with onions, since this will make them "cry their eyes out."

In past times, one corner of the garden or field was left wild, uncultivated. The rest of the land may have been vigorously weeded daily, but not that one spot. This "sacred corner" was left as an offering to unseen forces, for in those days, everyone knew of spirits and deities that have been forgotten today.

Perhaps this custom should be revived, for it reminds us of the powers of nature. Surely a few feet of land entangled with a wild profusion of plants (called "weeds" by the unenlightened) won't harm anyone, and it is a gentle reminder that the greatest cultivator of all is Nature.

11 The Garage

The garage is, arguably, the most neglected room of the house. When it's thought of at all, it's usually in purely practical terms—a place to keep the rain off your car, to store tools, to place the deep-freeze.

Both the garage and the cars we park in it may seem mundane but—guess what?—magic lies within them.

After all, the car is simply one of the latest vehicles we've created to speed ourselves around the world. It isn't far removed from the horse and buggy, ox cart or chariot. In a sense, the car is a portable "home" we take with us when we leave our residence behind.

The garage is the car's domain. It guards and protects it as much as the home does us. Beyond this, it can become one of the most magical rooms of the house—a temple room, an occult workshop or a magical stillroom.

In earlier times, horses did much of the work cars do today. All manner of amulets and charms were used to guard both the beast and the cart often attached to it. Bells were hung around the animal's neck to scare off evil spirits; shiny horse brasses were attached to reflect the evil eye and thus spare the creature from death; the tail and manes were braided, sometimes with red ribbon, to further guard the horse.

Carts have also been similarly protected. Vibrant paint and symbols such as eyes and crescent moons protected the cart from adversity. Until the last century, every carriage in Naples had one or more charms—usually horns or feathers—hanging from it. Gypsy wagons (which still exist today, although in rapidly diminishing numbers) are a prime example of a magically protected vehicle of yesterday that has retained its occult meaning and power.

Much of this was in the past, before the advent of the automobile. With it and the "shrinking globe" that efficient transportation has created, we've attained a larger world view.

But did such practices die out? Or, rather, has the human need for such charms left us?

No. We please ourselves by thinking that we are rational, materialistic human beings, but civilization paints a thin veneer on primitive emotions and feelings. Put us in a potentially life-threatening situation—driving a car, for example—and we lose some of our sophistication.

Look in any parking lot. You'll see religious symbols or statues in many cars, suspended from the rear-view mirror or mounted on the dashboard. These are appeals to higher powers to bless and guard the car.

After a wedding, cans are often tied to the rear bumper of the wedded pair's car. The purpose? As the car drives off, the cans' clangings magically exorcise negativity that might otherwise be attracted to the happy couple and cause an accident on their honeymoon night.

Today, the automobile is very much a superstition-ridden object. Washing a car inevitably brings rain; this has been "proven" quite often. A driver who boasts of an accident-free driving record might soon have a fender-bender for daring to tempt fate and the gods above. Some cars seem to be jinxed and never work right. A driver who has had good luck with a particular make or model will probably purchase a new car of the same type. Many owners name their cars, talk to them, see their unique personalities. To many, the car is more than a vehicle or a means of transportation—it's a living entity.

There are car owners among us who drive, eat, sleep, argue, make up, make out and sometimes even *live* in their cars. On such occasions, the car truly becomes a home and is subject to household magic.

Since the automobile of today is just as firmly lodged in the magic world as the horse and cart of 100 years ago, it makes sense to use magic to keep our cars operating correctly and protect them from accidents and theft. Thinking about it on a purely psychological level, if it helps us drive more safely, it works.

To bless and guard your car, start with the physical: Clean it from roof to tires, inside and out. In the final rinse water, add an infusion of a protective herb—such as *bay, rosemary* or *dill*—to spread its vibrations over the entire car. (To make an infusion, steep 1 tablespoon herb in one cup boiling water. Let steep for 10 minutes, strain and use.) If you have your car professionally cleaned, put the infusion in a spray bottle mixed with water, spray over the car and wipe it dry.

Next, perform a car-protection ritual, such as the following. (This spell can be done either in the garage or outside, in a place where you won't be seen.)

Assemble the following: four white candles or lanterns, a compass, salt and some frankincense or rose geranium oil. After parking your vehicle with its hood facing *East*, light one candle (or lantern) and place it about 1-1/2 feet from the radiator on the floor or ground. As you place the candle, imagine yourself weaving a web of protective energy—like a spider's web—around the car. Fashion it of glowing purple, blue or white light with your visualization.

As you light the second candle, walk to the *South*. You should have the passenger-side door to you. Place the candle down, still visualizing the web of light. Continue on to the *West* and *North* until four glowing candles sit all around the car and you.

Once this has been done, sprinkle salt onto the car's hood and roof and a little on the floor inside. Anoint the windows, doors and tires with *frankincense* or *rose geranium oil* (or some other protective scent) and get into the car. Let the candles burn for several minutes as you relax in the car, feeling the protective energies infused within. It is done.

Just as wagons were brightly painted in the past, so are cars similarly colored. Colors are powers and energies that are at the heart of a thousand spells; therefore, the color of your car is magically potent. It can be a powerful influence upon both your car and you.

Bright cars are more quickly noticed on the street; in magical thought, this might invite looks of jealousy or even violence against the vehicle itself. Police seem more likely to spot, and quite possibly ticket, a flashy red sports car—if they can catch it.

For something as important as a car, don't settle for a color you don't enjoy. If you want a yellow car, throw a paint job on that aqua jalopy. If you like it, you need please no one else.

Pinstriping and other decorations are quite popular today. Some vans have entire murals executed on one side, often with mythological themes (wizards, dragons, unicorns, etc.). Flames and skulls, eyes and other symbols are found riding along fenders or flaring out on hoods and doors. Such pictures are more than art; they are expressions of the owner's personality and serve to stamp the vehicle as a part of him or her. Certainly such symbols as flames, intertwining lines and skulls magically guard the vehicle, whether the driver in question is aware of it or not.

There are some highly popular car spells in use today. For an external car-protection spell, take about a tablespoon each of *rosemary, dill* and *basil*. Place this mixture in a small bag and put it in one of the hubcaps. The motion of the wheel will constantly charge the sachet with energy, and it will help protect your car.

Inside the car, there is a wealth of protective amulets that can be used. Such objects—charged with the task of guarding the vehicle from accidents, keeping it in running condition and protecting it against theft—have taken many forms. They can be hung from the rear-view mirror, placed on the dashboard, tucked inside the glove compartment or stuffed under the seat.

Use protective charms with which you feel comfortable. Religious images, as mentioned earlier, are popular, but you needn't limit yourself to them.

Quartz crystals are an excellent magical tool, ideally suited for car use. Obtain a small quartz crystal. While actually sitting in your parked car, hold it in one hand. Firmly visualize your car and all that will ever be within it guarded from danger. *See* your car bathed in a glow of magical, protective light—perhaps white or purple or electric blue. Visualize it remaining in perfect working order. When you have fully saturated the crystal, place it somewhere safe in the car. You may wish to make up a small cloth bag for the "point," or you can casually place it in the glove compartment or suspend it from the rear-view mirror. Many people wear quartz crystals as ritual or everyday jewelry. Why not one for your car?

Or, you might want to try the *Dinosaur Car Spell*. Buy

or make a small image of a ferocious, fear-inspiring creature. You could pick up a plastic stegosaurus from your
local toy store or carve a dragon from balsa wood and
detail it with poster paints.

Once it ismade or obtained, place the creature on your
car's dashboard, visualizing it as a living, breathing thing.
Give it life through your visualization. Send it energy, and it
will guard your car.

A vivid green dinosaur, sporting a bright red head now
faded with the sun, rides on Scott's dashboard. Its gaping
mouth, with carefully molded teeth, points toward traffic in
an endlessly protective gesture.

A clove of *garlic* placed somewhere in the car provides protection (as does a bag of *salt*), but unless you're a
diehard fan of the odoriferous bulb, I wouldn't recommend
using this in the car. Any red object, also traditionally effective, could be used in its place.

Sachets are another alternative. There are mixtures
blended specifically for use in the car. Sachets are easy to
make and can indeed help your car through some tough
spots. Mix up:

> *Comfrey* (for protection during travel)
> *Caraway* (for protection against theft)
> *Rosemary* (for protection against theft)
> *Ash* (for protection against accidents)
> *Mugwort* (for protection during travel)

Moisten with a few drops of one or all of the following:

> *Frankincense oil*
> *Rose geranium oil*
> *Aloe vera gel*

Mix and place in a red cloth square. Tie up into a bag with
red or white cord so that the herbs are trapped inside, and

place in your car. Squeeze every few days to infuse with power. Replace the sachet when the scent is gone.

Two herbs are hung separately from the rear-view mirror for specific reasons. Wormwood protects the car on dangerous roads, while plantain guards it against any negative energies that may travel the streets.

An Italian car charm: Take salt, a piece of palm leaf, a tiny gold horn and a small pair of scissors or a small knife. Place these in white cloth, tie the ends shut with red ribbon and place in the glove compartment for protection.

To enhance your own safety and that of your passengers in the car, dab some protective oil on the seat belts, and then wear them!

You may wish to cense your car at regular intervals. Burning incense within the car may seem like a strange idea, but it's quite logical. It improves your car's odor and clears it of negativity. For safety reasons, burn cone incense in the car's ashtray. Think of the ashtray as a censer. Pick a suitable scent (*frankincense, sandalwood* and *myrrh* are always good choices) and burn it with the windows rolled down while parked safely in the garage or on the street, or while driving down the road.

A few magical rules concerning driving are still observed today. One of the most common is that it is extremely unlucky to drive into a dust devil or whirlwind. Not only is it hard on your air filter and paint job, it also brings chaos and confusion into your life.

An all-purpose driving spell: On the day before starting out on a long trip by car, take a map of the area you'll be traveling through, three white candles, a length of white cord and a red pen or white ink and a dip pen. On a table or some other flat surface in your garage (if you have one), mark your journey on the map. (Make sure it's one you can leave at home.) Enclose the entire distance to be driven in circles of protective white or red ink.

Next, draw symbols of protection (such as stars) and life (ankhs) on the map and set three white candles burning around it so that they form a triangle totally encompassing your route. Let the candles burn for a few minutes while you visualize yourself and your companions (if any) making the journey safely.

Finally, pinch out the candle flames, roll up the map and tie it firmly with a white cord. Place it where it will not be found until you return home. At that time, slip off the cord without untying it and dispose of it and the map.

The garage—the car's "house"—is an important part of the magical household. In the past, vehicles were kept outside in sheds or huts, or even in the home, along with the cows and chickens and other animals. Things were cozy in those days.

Today, the garage is much more than a grease-stained, tool- and workbench-lined, open-raftered laundry room. It needs to be guarded and brought into the flow of the rest of the house if your home is expected to run smoothly.

If the garage isn't used to store any cars, it can be transformed into a room devoted solely or mostly to magic. More than one spell has been whipped up on a garage workbench. Runes have been carved, images formed and herbs mixed in the sight of hammers, nails and saws.

Put your imagination to work. An altar or magical spell table can be set up in the garage, supplies kept in cupboards and all manner of magic made within. Some people store their occult libraries in the garage if they are uncomfortable having such things in the house. (What would the neighbors say?)

For comfort's sake, the door can be permanently sealed

and waterproofed. A small heater can be installed. Carpets of magical design may be laid on the floor and thick curtains of pleasing colors hung at the windows to shut out the eyes of the curious.

A permanent or temporary magical altar, consisting of a cleared bench or table, can be set up. Sacred images or symbols, candles, an incense burner and your other magical tools can be laid out for use.

Inside your garage—with incense smouldering, candles flickering and a passage of magical flute music drifting from a hidden tape recorder—you are free to cast spells or compound mixtures to be used in your household magic.

If the garage is dry, warm and well ventilated, it is an ideal place to dry herbs for use in magic. Hang them from the rafters and allow them to dry naturally.

Even those uninterested in converting their garage into a magical temple should purify it, along with the rest of the house, at regular intervals. (See Chapter 14.) Also, most of the protective devices mentioned in this book can be placed within it to guard against the intrusion of unsavory people, such as robbers.

Carry a smoking censer into the garage once in a while to clear and align its energies with those of the rest of the house.

A *Garage Witch Bottle:* In any jar with a tight-fitting lid, place old rusted nails, screws, brads, bolts, nuts, staples, sharp pieces of wire, tacks and any other wicked or pointy things lying around in the garage.

Sweep the floor clean of all debris. Next, spread a few handfuls of salt over the floor, sweep this up and add to the jar.

Screw on the lid and walk around the garage, looking for the ideal place to put the bottle.

As you walk, chant the following or similar words:

Negativity
Extinguished be!
Negativity
Extinguished be!
Negativity
Extinguished be!

When the correct location for the Witch bottle becomes known to you, place it there and burn incense to seal the spell.

12   Protection

To truly be a place of magical living, the house must be secure from unwanted intrusions, both physical and non-physical. In the past, guarding against thieves was treated in the same way as warding off evil spirits and werewolves; though the "enemies" are different, they are similar in threat. Over millennia, we have sanctified certain objects, gestures, symbols and signs to act as bar and bolt against all that would harm us.

A home should be a place of refuge, security and warmth. It is of the utmost importance to retain these qualities. While alarms and dead-bolt locks do their part, our inner selves yearn for mystic charms woven by moonlight with words of power. These charms, placed inside or outside the home, ward off ghosts, demons, wraiths, curses and creatures from the abyss, as well as thieves and sales representatives.

There are many charms and spells you can use to safeguard your home. Choose those that speak to your sense of mystery and spark your imagination. These will be the most effective.

Amulets are objects that repel negative (evil) influences. They can be worn, carried, suspended from ceilings, concealed between walls, propped up on furniture or slipped behind family pictures. Household amulets guard the home by driving away harmful energies, thus ensuring a calm atmosphere within.

According to tradition, it is best to have at least three amulets in the house. They can be of identical or different types. Unless specified, place them in spots of prominence: near a household altar (see Chapter 19), on or near doors and windows, or near the hearth.

Stones with naturally occurring holes, called holey stones, can be found on beaches and in river beds throughout the world. Excellent household protectors, they can be hung singly from cords throughout the house, or several can be strung together on a thick cord like a necklace and hung behind the front door.

On a beach near San Diego where we often go, thundering waves toss up holed stones in great number and variety. Although these stones are excellent protective devices, try to *find* one for maximum effectiveness.

Agates and *lodestones* are both powerful household amulets. The larger the stones, the greater their effect. Lodestones (natural magnets) have long been used in magic, setting up fields of energy that screen out negative vibrations. Agates bring luck to the home, as does a carved piece of *turquoise*.

A stone amulet may consist of one or more of these types of stones placed in a white bag and tied with yarn. For greatest effect, mix the stones.

Fossils, owing to their tremendous age and eerie appearance, have long been called upon to guard the home. Generally placed on window sills or hearths, or suspended from beams, fossils bring luck and guard against the effects of bad weather, according to ancient magical tradition. Choose fossils that appeal to you; those marked with stars, such as sand dollars, work doubly well.

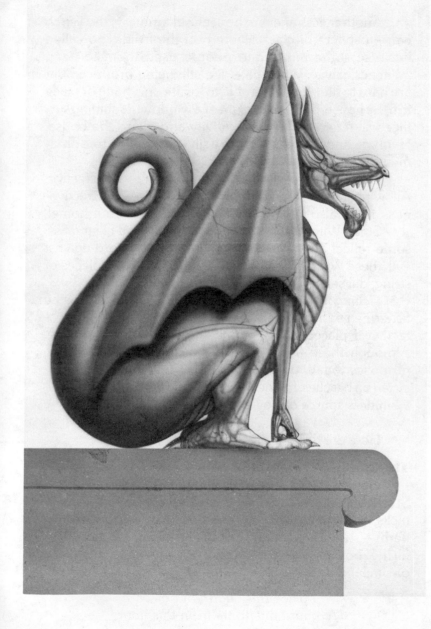

Another, less ancient, household amulet is the *Witch ball*—a sphere of glass silvered on the inside. So called because some misguided people used them to keep "Witches" away, Witch balls are still being produced but are hard to find. If you are able to locate one, hang or place it in the house, perhaps in front of a window. Its shining surface will reflect evil and negativity and guard the house. Until you find one, you can use a silver glass Yule tree ornament instead.

The Witch ball should be kept clean to be effective. Allowing it to become dirty not only negates its effectiveness, it can also pull negative vibrations into your home!

Some Witch balls are made of unsilvered clear glass; some reflect a swirl of different colors. To guard against evil, these Witch globes are often filled with tiny pieces of string, dill seed or pins.

Fishing floats, spheres of colored glass once used by fishermen to float nets, are also thought to be highly protective if placed in the home or hung in nets outside. Although these floats are manufactured for decorative purposes today, the most effective ones are those collected on beaches, for they were actually used in the ocean—a limitless source of power.

Here are three protective charms:

The Shoe

Obtain an old shoe, preferably one made of leather. Stuff it with protective objects, such as pins, needles, nails, tacks, scissors and bits of broken glass. Add protective herbs—such as rosemary, basil, fern, bay or mistletoe—to fill the shoe. Hang it in the attic or basement, saying these or similar words:

> *I place this charm of power*
> *To guard my home from this hour.*

The Bottle

Find a large bottle and stuff it with small pieces of thread of many colors (except black). This project will probably take you many weeks, since only small pieces of thread (one to three inches in length) should be used, and each must be introduced into the bottle separately.

As you add each piece of thread, say something like the following:

> *Tangle the bane up!*
> *Tangle the bane up!*
> *Tangle the bane up!*

When the bottle is full, cap and place it in a window, in the attic or in a cupboard.

A Witch's Bottle

Gather rosemary, needles and pins. Fill a small jar with these three ingredients, saying the following as you work:

> *Pins, needles, rosemary, wine*
> *In this Witch's bottle of mine;*
> *Guard against harm and enmity;*
> *This is my will, so mote it be!*

Visualize these herbs doing just that. When the jar is full, pour in red wine. Then cap or cork the jar and drip wax from a black or red candle around the seal. Bury the jar at the farthest corner of your property or place it in an inconspicuous spot in the house. The Witch's bottle destroys negativity and evil: The pins and needles impale evil, the wine drowns it, and the rosemary sends it far from your property.

Protection sachets are another way in which herbs are often used in guarding the house. Sachets are mixtures of herbs and flowers that are tied in cloth and hung or placed to release the plants' powers and scents to do their magic.

Three of the basic types of home-protection sachets can be made according to the following instructions:

All-Purpose Protection Sachet
>Rosemary
>Basil
>Dill

Place these dried herbs in a piece of red or white cloth. Tie up the bundle with red yarn and hang it over the front door (or as close as possible), saying protective words and visualizing.

Anti-Theft Sachet
>Caraway
>Rosemary
>Juniper
>Elder (or mistletoe)

Place these ingredients in a piece of white cloth, tie it up with white yarn and hang it prominently in your home, visualizing the sachet barring the entrance of thieves.

Weather-Protection Sachet
>Cedar
>Mistletoe
>Bay

Place these three items in a piece of white cloth. Tie it together with white yarn and hang it in the highest place in the house, or the chimney.

If you wish to place some household protectants outdoors, there are many spells you can use. One of the most picturesque involves putting an earthenware image of a lion or cat on the roof, situated where it can be plainly seen from the street.

Remember: While performing any such magical act, use your powers of concentration and visualization to back up your physical efforts. A clay lion on your roof won't, by itself, be effective. But an earthenware lion that you have visualized with protective purple energy streaming from its eyes—which you can see in your magical imagination stirring, rising to its legs and keeping watch over your property—will be more magically potent.

A similar charm: Obtain a statue of a lion, griffin or dragon and place it on your front porch or the steps leading up to it. These creatures are extremely protective and have been used for centuries. Today, many libraries and other public buildings continue this practice without knowing its magical background.

You might wish to obtain several small lengths of bamboo. By the light of the Sun at noon, carve protective symbols (pentagrams, hearts, crosses) on the sticks and thrust them into the ground around the house. Do this "with power," of course, visualizing as you plant the sticks that you are creating a curtain of protective energy about your house.

A concave mirror hung on the outside of your home will deflect any evil that may come to it from the house across the street. Also, placing small mirrors facing outward in the windows is effective.

Scattering rice on your roof diffuses any evil forces that may have been sent to your home, but it also may attract pests. If this is a problem, try substituting sand for the rice.

An old American Indian spell consists of planting a cactus at each corner of your house's foundation. (All of the cacti should be of the same variety.) This guards against the entrance of unwanted influences and powers.

Whitewashing a house to protect it from evil has long

been considered highly effective. This is a rather drastic measure, however, because the whitewash must not be allowed to become dirty or discolored.

S-shaped shutter holders keep evil from a house, as do the cruciate or s-shaped braces that are often attached to the walls of old houses.

Finally, obtain a small tube and place three arrows inside it. Deposit this on your roof, and it will guard against evil.

As discussed earlier, herbs are popular household protectants. Try the following recipe for more herbal protection.

Take equal parts of the following:

> Basil
> Elder
> Valerian
> Marjoram

Using your hands and working over a bowl, squeeze these herbs into a powder. Now walk through the house, moving clockwise from room to room, scattering the herb powder lightly so that it is evenly spread in every room. This will bring protection, good fortune, peace and security from attackers and thieves.

Hazelnuts strung on a red cord and hung in the home bring luck and money, but don't be tempted to eat one of the nuts. A rod of hazel wood hung in the home is also protective. Hazelnut necklaces, found in prehistoric tombs, might have been used for protective purposes even back then.

A sprig of *mistletoe* hung from the ceiling protects the home against hostile spirits, while *garlic* placed in a window sill guards against thieves.

And finally, if you become nervous or scared when descending steps into a basement or traveling up a long flight of steps into a musty, shadow-ridden attic, place a sprig of *rue* at the foot of the stairs.

Your fears should vanish.

13   By Broom and Rag

Cleaning the house may not seem like too mystical a task, but here again magic rears its unpredictable head. Keeping in mind the magical element of household chores may help you whip up more enthusiasm as you reach for the broom, mop or rag. If not, at least you'll have something interesting to think about while sweeping and scrubbing— the mysterious powers that the ancients saw at work in these actions.

The broom has long been associated with magic, probably due to its shape, use in purification rites and kinship with magical wands and staffs. The common household tool is so sacred that, in some parts of the world, broom deities exist.

In China, the broom goddess is *Sao Ch'ing Niang*, or *Sao Ch'ing Niang-Niang*. Known as the Lady with the Broom, she lives on the Broom Star, *Sao Chou*, and presides over good weather. When rain continues too long, threatening crops, farmers cut out paper images of brooms and paste them on their doors or fences to bring clear weather and sunshine. These images invoke the Lady with the Broom.

In pre-Columbian Mexico, the Aztecs worshiped the Witch-Goddess *Tlazolteotl*, who was usually depicted car-

113

rying or riding a broom. In her rites, priests burned black incense and laid brooms made from rushes (symbolizing the Goddess) across the fire. Owls, snakes and the Moon were also dedicated to *Tlazolteotl*. The Goddess was invoked to sweep away the worshipers' transgressions.

In the old days, several different types of brooms were specially prepared for use in magic. For other than normal sweeping spells, you should have one broom in your house reserved for magic and ensure it isn't used for anything else. In a pinch, however, the everyday household broom can be used in magical spells.

There are many associations made between brooms and Witches, some of them off-color and all confused. Witches didn't fly on broomsticks, of course, but, like their accusers, they did use them to clean their cottages. Reports that Witches galloped around on broomsticks during their ritual dances may hold some truth, but that was nothing shocking a few hundred years ago. And to this day, some folks give their children hobby-horses.

The magic of the broom wasn't limited to the Witch and her kin; everyone practiced magic a few generations ago. Some of these broom-related spells persist today. For instance, many people believe that moving an old broom to a new house will bring the worst of fortunes. Making a wish when a new broom is first used, however, will cause the wish to come true through the magic of the tool.

If a broom falls from your hands while you sweep, make a wish before retrieving it. And anyone who desires to be married merely has to jump over a broom nine times; within a year, he or she will be signing the license.

To bring rain, stand outside and swing a broom in the air over your head. When a lightning storm blows your way, think about putting your broom on the porch to act as a lightning rod; electricity and lightning are thought to be attracted to brooms. Another way to safeguard a house against strikes involves crossing a spade and a broom outside the main entrance to the house.

One old wart cure (there are thousands) consists of measuring a wart crosswise with a broomstraw, then burying the straw. The straw, so intimately connected with the wart, will decay, and so too should the blemish. This ancient practice of "taking the measure" is related to image magic.

Placing a broom across any doorway allows your departed friends and family to speak to you if they so choose. As long as the broom remains in place, they can communicate freely. This practice obviously relates to the power of the door as a threshold into other worlds.

The broom has been used for protective purposes as well. Babies and small children were long thought to be susceptible to psychic and other forms of attack. Placing a small broom beneath their pillows was thought to keep evil far from their slumbers.

Two brooms crossed and hung on a wall or nailed to a door guard the house, as does a broom placed on the ground before a door. The brooms are believed to disperse negative energies before they can bother you.

Take two needles, make an equal-armed cross with them and place the cross in a broom. Stand the broom behind a door, and it will guard your home. (By the way, when standing a broom in a corner, put it bristles up, handle to the floor. This not only ensures that the bristles will last longer, it also brings good luck.)

If you feel you are being followed and haunted by unfriendly ghosts, stepping over a broomstick will prevent them from disturbing you.

When nightmares are a problem, let a broom sweep them away. Hang one on the bedroom door and place garlic beneath your pillow. You should sleep peacefully.

Sweeping spells are quite ancient. For instance, a new broom should be used to sweep something *into* the house before it sweeps dirt out. If not, your luck will go out the door.

Buy a brand new broom, or better still, make one. Before using it for normal household sweeping, carve or write on its handle (the words running from the tip to the bristles on one side): "I sweep in money and luck." On the other side (with the words traveling away from the bristles), carve or write: "I sweep out evil and poverty." Visualize as you clean the floors, and you'll do just that.

Many people will not sweep floors at night because doing so is said to prevent good fortune. This belief seems to be based on the ancient folklore that says sweeping disturbs the spirits of the deceased who walk the floors while the rest of us sleep.

When sweeping, remember to do so *toward* the fireplace, if you have one. If not, sweep in any direction except toward the front door. If you ignore this warning, you might remove your house's luck.

Broom magic, no matter how rich and colorful, doesn't constitute the entire art of cleansing magic. The act of spring cleaning, a long-established ritual, also has magical overtones. Spring is the time of the Earth's renewal, a rousing of nature after the cold sleep of winter. As such, it is an ideal time to clean your home—to welcome in the energies of the new season.

Spring cleaning is more than physical work; it should also involve a concentrated effort on your part to rid yourself of the problems and negativity of the past months and prepare yourself for the coming spring and summer.

Approach the task of cleaning your house with positive thoughts and a sense of the magical aspects of your work: You are freeing your home of the harsh energies of winter.

Cleansing it physically, you are preparing it for the ritual purification that should follow. (See Chapter 14.)

Legend has it that any spring cleaning performed after the end of May will have no effect; indeed, June is rather late for tackling spring chores.

You may wish to begin your spring cleaning with this brief ritual: Open the windows to air out the house. Light a white candle, anoint it with a fresh, floral-scented oil (such as rose), place a flower or sprig of fragrant leaves before this and meditate for a few moments on your coming activities. Visualize yourself psychically purging the house, washing it clean. Then, while the candle continues to burn, begin your chores.

There is some lore and magic concerning mops, though it is limited compared to that of brooms. For example, if you hang a mop outside your back door, no spells can be cast against you. Just don't do any mopping with it, or buy a second mop to use, if you try this spell.

It's also said to be "bad luck" to step over a mop (especially if you trip while doing it). It's far luckier to pick the thing up than ignore it and risk an accident.

All household work—from scrubbing stains in the kitchen sink to swabbing the floor with a mop to polishing wood furniture—should be done with clockwise motions. This practice imbues your work, and the object you're cleaning, with positive energy.

Dishrags seem to have their own particular brand of magic. It's said to be good luck to steal a dishrag from a neighbor, but I don't recommend this. I'd assume it means you'll share in your neighbor's good times as well as bad, which is certainly good luck for your neighbor.

Your own dishrags can bring you fortune as well. The next time it rains, hang one outside to receive the liquid blessings. Or, bury one outdoors by the light of the Full Moon. Both actions are thought to be lucky.

Like brooms, dishrags should never be moved from one house to another. Why take that old dirt with you when you can leave it behind?

Finally, here's an old country spell: If your best table-cloth is stained and no normal laundering process will clean it, take it outside when the Full Moon is shining overhead. Spread it out on the lawn or drape it over soft-leaved bushes and leave it there until dawn. The Moon's pale white rays will whiten the cloth as you sleep.

14   Household Purifications

No matter how carefully you clean your home, no matter how often you vacuum, mop, shine, dust and polish, there may be "dirt" that your brushes and cloths won't remove.

Every house is subject to negative energies—angry thoughts, fear, chaos—that seep in through the cracks in the walls, are broadcast via satellite to our television sets and radios and are stirred wherever humans live.

But don't get paranoid about this; no nasty creatures are going to pop out from your toaster to terrorize you in the dark. The negativity is just that—negative vibrations that are without form but that are very real on other levels of existence and can affect our lives on this one.

Negativity weighing down on any house can strain relationships, create tension, increase arguments and accidents and ruin a good party. It may also prevent sleep and cause the whole house to assume a heavy, malignant atmosphere. When this happens, purify the home of the negativity that is unavoidably attracted to it.

Monthly household purifications will drastically reduce the negativity in your home. If you live far from an urban area, you might perform household purifications every three months or so, or when tempers seem to flare. It's best to per-

119

form these purifications during the waning Moon (when the Moon shrivels from a glowing white orb to an invisible globe). If the need arises, however, don't wait for the proper Moon phase—just do it. Rituals, after all, aren't holy writ.

Purifications drive away general negativity, the kind that abounds in cities and apartment buildings. However, a purification is *not* an exorcism; it won't rid a place of troublesome spirits. Likewise, though purifications are generally successful, they are no defense against a conscious direction of negative energy toward you. Protective magic and rituals designed to direct the energy back to the sender—utilizing candles, mirrors, iron, salt, herbs, quartz crystals, baths, incenses and a pantry-full of other tools—perform this function, as do exorcisms. Several of the protective spells and rites mentioned in this book will help you defend yourself in such situations, as will any personal-protection spells, amulets and talismans in your possession.

O.K., let's get to the point here. We mentioned a "conscious direction of negative energy" above. This means a curse or hex. Just the mention of these is usually enough to convince some people that they've been subjected to one. After all, it's easier to blame our life problems on outside influences, thereby releasing ourselves of responsibility for our progress or guilt about our mistakes.

If the idea of curses and hexes upsets you, relax. They are rare. Most people who believe that something like this has happened to them have been "cursed" with a vivid but untrained imagination. Even when harmful spells are cast, they aren't usually effective. Because they are performed without our consent, they must get through our natural psychic armor before they can affect us.

So, what can we do to keep our magical self-defense systems fully operational? Stay healthy. Exercise moderately. Maintain a positive attitude toward life and believe in your

own powers and abilities. Take full responsibility for your past and future actions. Perform regular self-protection magic and back this up with concentration and visualization.

Sadly, thanks to decades of entertaining but misleading novels and movies, many people are terrified of falling under another's magic power. This fear may ruin a person's mental and physical health; thus, the nonexistent "curse" actually has an effect!

Even if no spells have been cast, people who wish to blame a curse for their troubles will point smugly to the "evidence." "See? You didn't believe me. Now I'm losing weight, my hair's falling out and I eat raw meat at dawn. That *proves* I've been hexed!"

Absurd, yes, but all too often true. If you think you're sick, chances are you'll soon show symptoms. This isn't simply psychological; it's magical. *Thoughts are things.*

So keep healthy and sane. In the unlikely event that someone does attempt to cast a spell on you, you won't be an easy target. The steady flow of positive energies circulating throughout your house will further protect you, which leads us back to the subject of household purifications.

To begin, open all windows and doors to allow the negativity to easily vacate your house. The act of opening up your house at the very least replaces the stale air with fresh. It is also part of the ritual of purification and is symbolic of your intention to clean the house. Fresh air and sunshine also help sweep and burn away negativity.

As with most magical deeds, household purification must be backed up with physical work; thus, a purification of the house begins with scrubbing the floors and washing the windows. Because like attracts like, dirty, unkempt houses—with no order whatsoever—practically invite disturbing vibrations. Even if your home isn't scrupulously neat, it's in order if you know where everything is.

While cleaning the house, see yourself washing away all the sorrows and problems that have accumulated there. Even if you are unable to see or sense them, imagine their presence anyway. See the dirt in the water (on the sponge or mop) as containing that negativity. Immediately dispose of such contaminated water outside. After vacuuming, remove the bag, take it outside and replace it with a fresh one.

Once the house is physically clean, you are ready to start the magical purification. Any of the following rituals can be used. Though they vary greatly, they are similar in intent. Choose one that appeals to you and repeat it regularly to ensure that your magical household truly remains "home sweet home."

The Elemental Purification

This rite utilizes the powers of the four elements (Earth, Air, Fire, Water) to cleanse the home. At a time when you are alone in the home, or in the presence of family members or housemates, assemble on a table the following items:

A bowl or flat dish of salt
An incense burner (censer)
Frankincense (or any other sweet-fumed incense
    sticks, cones or powder)
A white candle
A bowl of clean, pure water

Light the incense and the candle. Stand before the table and open yourself to your home. Feel its energies. Really tune in to any impressions you receive.

After a moment, hold your hands over the assembled tools and say something like the following (feel free to improvise):

I charge you, tools of the elements,
To sweep my house clean of all ill and bane.
This is my will, so mote it be!

Take the dish of salt and, moving *clockwise* around the house, throw a pinch of salt into each corner of every room, saying the following or similar words:

By the powers of Earth, I cleanse this house!

In your imagination, see the salt burning away negativity as you sprinkle and toss it. Your purification will be as strong as your visualization.

Also throw pinches into cupboards and closets, through open windows and doors, into attics and basements, and in the garage.

Next, set the salt down and pick up the censer. While the incense smokes, carry it on the same route you used with the salt. Holding it before open windows and doors and in the corners of each room, visualize the smoke clearing away all negativity and evil. Say the following at regular intervals:

By the powers of Air, I cleanse this house!

Once you have walked through the whole house, return the censer and take the lit candle on the same route. Again, visualize, moving clockwise and holding the flame before windows and doors, seeing it shining forth with magical power, burning away negativity. Every so often, say:

By the powers of Fire, I cleanse this house!

Finally, replace the candle on the table and take up the bowl of water. Sprinkle water throughout the house, in every corner and at exits and entrances. Toss some drops at and through windows. *See* and *know* that the water is washing away ills with a tidal wave of magical power. Say the following:

By the powers of Water, I cleanse this house!

Set the bowl on the table and stand for a few minutes in the house. It should feel calmer, more peaceful, fresh and clean. If not, repeat the ritual.

Close the doors and windows, and, if time permits, leave the salt, incense, candle and water together on the table until the candle burns itself out and the incense is reduced to ash.

The Broom Purification

Before dawn, take a branch from any tree. Thank the tree for its gift and leave a coin or semiprecious stone at its base in payment.

Next, obtain several brightly colored flowers on long stalks. Tie these flowers to the branch to fashion a sort of broom, then sweep the floor in every room of the house, visualizing the flowers of the broom absorbing negativity and "evil" as you work. Then, still before sunrise, leave the broom at a crossroads. Traditionally in the Southwest United States and Mexico, this ritual is repeated at the first of each month.

The Infusion Purification

Collect equal parts (about a handful each) of dried *marjoram, bay* and *rosemary.* Heat a gallon of water until it is almost boiling, remove it from the heat and toss the herbs into the water. Cover and allow to cool.

Strain the herbs from the water and, using your fingers, sprinkle the infusion throughout the house. Move in a clockwise direction, visualizing and saying something like the following:

> *I banish evil and negativity;*
> *This is my will, so mote it be.*

Touch the water to doors and windows, appliances and furniture, outside around the home and on the surrounding property. Be sure to pour some down the drains as well. Visualize the water cleansing the whole area. It is done.

The Lemon Infusion

When the Moon is full, completely peel nine lemons using your hands alone. As you finish peeling each one, place the peels in a bucket or a large bowl of water.

Next, gently squeeze the peels into the water, expressing their oils until the sharp, clean fragrance of lemon hangs heavily in the air. Visualize the lemons' powers cleansing your home of negativity.

Next, still visualizing, scrub the floors, doorknobs and windows with the lemon water. Pour a little of the remaining water down each drain. Repeat this ritual each Full Moon.

15 Moving

Moving from one home to another is a time of turmoil—a rustling of old energies and sparking of new ones. Not only do our surroundings change, but the energies of the new house are usually quite different as well.

To smooth the transition, you can perform spells to ritually end your residence at one place and begin your new one elsewhere. Such rites have been used for thousands of years, some by people who are not remotely aware of their origins in ancient Pagan magic.

One belief is that the conditions on your moving day magically forecast your future in the new residence. The weather is considered an important factor; for instance, if you move during a snowstorm, you will gain much money and great prosperity in your new home. A move during the waxing Moon ensures that your provisions will increase within it, while a rainy moving day signals much emotion.

The day of the week was once thought important too, due to planetary influences. Moving on a *Monday* is thought to bring you fewer nightmares and increase psychic awareness. A *Tuesday* move bestows sharper perception and intellectual powers to those in the house, while *Wednesday* moving raises passions of all kinds. If a *Thursday* is chosen

127

for the relocation, money will flow in through the front door, while a *Friday* move marks the existence of much love in the new home and a harmonious atmosphere.

Moves performed on *Saturday* are sometimes thought of as "bad luck," but this isn't so. In fact, it's a fine day to move into an older building or house. A *Sunday* move promises that all actions in the new home will prosper, good luck will flow into the house, and the light of reason will shine within it.

Before moving any possessions into a new home, perform a purification upon it. If this is impossible before the move, do it as soon as circumstances allow. Use one of the purification rites in Chapter 14, or devise your own.

There are a few magical rules concerning the act of moving itself. When vacating a house, always leave some money inside it, no matter how small an amount. Doing so brings good luck to you as well as to the next tenants.

Also before moving to your new home, place a bit of dirt from your former property in your shoes. Leave it there until you are in the new place, and good times will be had within it.

Another spell to ensure good luck is to take a slip, cutting or bulb from a plant at the old house and place it in your new garden. (Moving house plants from the old place to the new satisfies this custom.)

The first things brought into the new house are of magical importance. Several items in particular are thought to bring good luck. Some people bring salt and bread before anything else. With the salt representing wealth and the bread food, the new household should never know hunger or lack of money. Anciently, this was an offering to the *Lares*—the family household spirits of Roman times. Following the same idea, a basket overflowing with edi-

ble items—such as fruits, vegetables, nuts, bread and cheese —should be taken into the house first. To maintain stability in the new household, an item that cannot be blown away by the wind, such as a sturdy chair, should be among the first carried in.

There is one ancient rule that is rarely argued: Never move a broom from one house to another. It will bring your last residence's bad luck and dirt to your new home. (This doesn't pertain to decorative brooms or those reserved solely for magical use, only those actually used to sweep floors.) If, for some reason, you must move an ordinary broom, put it into the new house through an open window, and the ill luck will be deterred.

If you experience a delay in moving your possessions into your new home, cross a new mop and broom on its doorstep. Assuming the broom and mop have never been used, this practice will guard the home until you can move in.

On the day you take up residence in your new home, throw a handful of salt into the house upon first entering it. Also, open a shutter that faces East (if there is one), and the home will be guarded against destruction from storms.

To attune yourself to your new home's energies, light a blue or white candle and some sweet-smelling incense, and sit in silent meditation—expanding your consciousness to include the entire structure. Think your way through the house. Take a sensory tour of the place as you sit peacefully meditating. You might choose to say a few words to the house, or simply visualize your new home life as you want it to be.

As you unpack boxes and rearrange furniture, remember to fashion some home-protection charms or cast a few spells to ensure your home's security. If you have made sachets and charms for your previous home, it's best to bury them and make new ones rather than move them to your new home. But do what seems right. You may decide to keep your Witch ball or holed stone but make up a new bag of herbs and scatter the spent herbs onto the Earth.

Once you have moved, consider having a house-warming party. Aside from an excuse to have friends over, this is an excellent way to introduce your friends and new house to each other. Tradition says that if your guests bring gifts, they should be for the home, not for you. The most "holy" of these gifts are those used to maintain the building itself.

Just as you cleanse a new home before moving in, the one you leave behind should be similarly purified. In a sense, this is "putting the house to rest"—dispersing the energies that made it uniquely yours while you inhabited it. Similar rituals were used by our ancestors, and such spells ritually signal the end of your residence.

In the midst of a hectic, frantic move, such a rite may be necessarily limited to a few actions or words. However, with a little planning, you can leave enough time to perform a purifying ritual on your old house as soon as the last of your belongings are out. This ritual may be as simple as swinging your old broom over your head three times in each room, or taking the last sweepings and flinging them into the air as you visualize your psychic essence dissolving inside the home.

A culinary moving spell can also be performed. As close as possible to your move date, make something edible—bread, cake, pizza, etc.—in the shape of a house. (You must mix, bake and consume it in the house itself.) As you mix the batter or dough, pour into it the sum of the house's vibrations. (If negative ones are present, perform a purification first.)

Use any method you like to create your "edible house." Dough can be molded or sheet cakes cut out and iced to form the correct shape. House-shaped cookie cutters can also be used. Whatever you do, eat your "edible" house just before moving, and you will take a part of the real house's essence with you.

In a similar moving spell, fill an earthenware or glass vessel with salt. Walk through your old house with this jar, visualizing the salt absorbing the memories, joys, sorrows, experiences and all that has made the house a unique part of your life. Poke the bottle into closets, the garage and so on. Watch as the house is slowly purified of all negative energies, leaving it fresh and new for its next residents.

When the house is clean, take the bottle outside, cap or cork it tightly, seal it with melted wax (use a red crayon) and mark a protective symbol (a pentagram) on the bottle. Then take it to a wild place, bury it in the earth and don't look back as you leave.

Though we leave behind the energies of our past homes, there's no reason to try to block out the memories. Homes become part of us, and when we leave them behind, we leave a bit of ourselves with them.

So recall the good times and go about setting up a brand new magical household in your new residence. In no time at all, you'll feel right at home.

16   The Magical Year

The magical household feels the effects of the seasons as much as humans do. Household ritual practices are associated with the seasons and many ancient festivals. By following these customs, you can attune your home to the seasons and the powers behind them.

Let's start our magical year at *Yule*, on or about December 21.* This ancient Pagan holiday once commemorated the births of such solar deities as Mithras; only later did it come to be one of the most holy days of the Christian ritual calendar.

The Pagan customs and origins of Yule run deep, and few homes show no sign of change near the end of December. One of the most common customs, of course, is to bring a fir or pine tree indoors, where it is then decorated.

Many other magical activities can be done at this time of year. In earlier times, one of the most important was the Yule bonfire. This sacred blaze was built to give power and life to the Sun, which was thought of as being reborn at the Winter Solstice.

_____

* For exact dates of these holidays, see *Llewellyn's Astrological Calendar*.

In later times, the fire was tamed and brought indoors in the form of the Yule log. A huge limb was selected, dragged to the house and prepared for use. Carvings of suns, figures of men and other magical symbols were etched onto its surface, and it was sometimes decorated with greens.

If you wish to burn a Yule log, why not decorate it? Whip melted paraffin with a hand beater until fluffy but spreadable. Use dabs of this on the log to secure fir and cedar boughs, pine cones, mistletoe, rosemary, holly or other greens.

Along with the remnants of last year's log (if available), set it ablaze on the evening before Yule. Ensure that it will burn until morning. Best of all is a huge log that will continue to burn for three days or more, but not many fireplaces can accommodate such a monster. As you sit at the hearth watching the fire, sip cider or ale—traditional beverages on this night.

If you don't have a fireplace, you can make a Yule candle. Buy the largest, fattest red candle you can find. (Or better yet, make one.) With an ice pick, carve a figure of a blazing sun on the side of the candle, then place it in a holder or on a heat-proof tray. Ring its base with holly, pine, mistletoe, cedar, rosemary, bay, juniper and other evergreen plants. Burn the candle on Yule evening. If you want it to burn all night, place it in a cauldron or a large bowl and ring the cauldron itself with the greens.

Placing holly, mistletoe and a tree in the house during the Yule season brings the essence of nature and the wilderness inside during the darkest months of the year. It refreshes the home's energies and reminds us of the continuing growth and life of the Earth.

Placing candles or lights on the tree ensures that the household will have a year of plenty, warmth and light. For decorations, you might wish to forego the usual glass orna-

ments (the silver ones are miniature Witch balls) and hang oranges, apples and beribboned nuts from its boughs, as was the custom in years past. Garlands of popcorn and cranberries are also good natural touches and lend their herbal magic to the tree. Fragrant garlands made by stringing dried rosebuds and cinnamon sticks together add a nostalgic scent to the tree.

There are a few rules about domestic behavior on Yule. First of all, don't do any excessive work. If you enjoy handicrafts, refrain from spinning on Yule. Tradition says that no one should sit before the wheel or take up the spindle on December 21.

Eating an apple on Yule night ensures good health for the coming year, while a magical cleansing bath shrugs off the past six months' worries and troubles. Mix pine, bay and rosemary, tie them in cheesecloth, add them to the tub and soak.

New Year's Eve and New Year's Day are other times steeped in household magic, most of which ensures that the home and its residents will have a safe, comfortable, plentiful year.

There are many traditional New Year's Eve rituals. Burning seven candles on this night brings household luck. If you want more than luck, light a candle on each side of a mirror five minutes before midnight on New Year's Eve. Then look into the glass, and you'll see a vision.

A few minutes before midnight on the eve of the new year, open the doors and windows for a few minutes to release any negative vibrations from last year.

New Year's Eve is also an excellent time to increase your beauty. At midnight, wash your face in well water, look into a mirror by candlelight, and you will improve your appearance.

If you have a fireplace, you might want to try this spell.

To be rid of last year's banes and pains, bind your now-obsolete calendar with wool yarn. Place it in a hot fire while chanting:

> *Burn, burn, you day-book burn;*
> *Last year's worries ne'er return!*

The preceding rituals are simple to follow, but some are more complex. At one time in Scotland, each resident of the household washed his or her entire body in water into which three live embers from the household fire had been placed. Next, clean clothing was donned, the house thoroughly scrubbed, every lock opened and a shiny knife left near the front door. A light burning in the window all night topped off the ritual.

On New Year's Day itself, there is much to do in the way of good-luck rituals. First off, ensure that your pockets and cupboards are full on this day; that way, you'll have money all year. If you have greens in the house on New Year's Day, you'll have plenty of "green" cash during the following 12 months.

Juniper incense—or dried, crumbled juniper burned on charcoal blocks—ritually cleanses the home and is highly traditional. Grass and water can also be brought into the home to ensure plenty of food and drink.

Burning *bayberry* candles is a pleasantly scented custom. An old poem goes:

> *Bayberry candles, when burned to the socket,*
> *Bring luck to the home and gold to the pocket.*

Since you must let them burn down all the way, choose small tapers and place them in fireproof holders.

On New Year's Day, *not before*, it is permissible to hang up new calendars and almanacs.

The next magical holiday, February 2, was once known

as *Imbolc, Oimelc, Candlemas* and by numerous other names. It is well known in the United States as *Ground-hog Day.*

Imbolc celebrates the return of the Sun after winter. On this night, which the Romans dedicated to Venus, all the candles in the house were lit and torches carried out-side to welcome the return of the Sun. This custom can be followed today by briefly turning on all the lights in the house or lighting a candle in each room. A blazing fireplace is also highly appropriate.

On the 14th of February, *Valentine's Day,* lettuce and peas are supposed to be planted in the garden. To spread loving energies through your home on this occasion, light seven pink candles and a floral incense while visualizing your house flooded with this emotion. This is also an ex-cellent time to perform divinations to discover future loves or to simply cast love spells.

March often marks the start of spring cleaning. Bring the first flowers from the garden inside and open the win-dows to purify the house of its wintry isolation. If you have a garden, start working the ground as soon as the danger of frost has passed (which may be a month or so yet). As you plant, think magical thoughts. Visualize the seeds you're planting as they'll be when grown—strong, tall, healthy. Guard the patches with stones marked with pentagrams placed at strategic angles, the stars facing down so they won't attract attention.

Sometime in the spring, take a magical cleansing bath containing *marjoram* and *thyme.* Purifications and cleans-ings of the house in general are well suited to the spring, as are household projects such as repairing, painting and re-modeling. Before remodeling, leave an offering to the house and let it know what you're about to do.

On March 21 or thereabouts (the astronomical date

changes yearly), the Vernal Equinox is celebrated. In days past, eggs—symbols of life—were colored yellow and gold, then exchanged as gifts or used in ritual in honor of the Sun and fecundity deities, such as Eostra.

Fortunately, the custom of coloring eggs has survived. If you decide to do this, you might wish to use natural dyes. Beet juice, onion skins, grape juice and other plant materials produce beautiful dyes and are far more magical than the store-bought dye tablets.

To celebrate the Equinox, half fill a large bowl with water and place a selection of flowers in it. These can be annuals or perennials from your garden, wildflowers collected on a walk or fresh blooms from the florist shop. Set the bowl in a position of prominence in your home.

If you wish to improve your health throughout the coming year, drink cold water on the Vernal Equinox and eat a leaf of sage.

Also on March 21, sort through your personal possessions and weed out any clothing or other items that no longer suit you. Don't throw them away, though; donate them to charity.

May 1 was celebrated as *Beltane* in earlier times and still is today by Pagans and Witches. It is based in part on the old Roman festival of Floralia, dedicated to Flora, Goddess of Flowers. Many more know it as *May Day*. A wealth of customs and rites has survived from early times.

May Day was also the date the Romans honored the *Lares*, or household and family guardians. Wreaths were hung before their altars, incense burned and the family attuned to its spiritual essence.

Lilacs and *hawthorn* are traditionally brought into the home on May Day, which is unusual because both plants are generally viewed as ill-luck bringers in the house. On this day, though, the spell is broken.

The flowers of May—*bluebells, yellow cowslips, daisies, roses, marigolds, primroses* and hundreds of others are still brought inside to release their powers and connect the home with the living world outdoors.

To guard your home against the intense magical powers at work on Beltane, mark a cross in the hearth ashes with a *hazel twig*, or carry *elder twigs* three times around the house, then hang them up inside or place outside over the door.

At dawn on May Day, go to a garden or out in the woods and gather dew from plants, flowers and grass. Bathe your face in this dew, and it will highlight your beauty.

It is considered unfortunate to give away fire or salt on May Day, since these were at one time the two most sacred substances. Thus, give them away on May Day, and you give your luck away.

Beltane marks the beginning of summer, when all nature reaches a crescendo of power and energy. The day and night were thought to be dangerous for the unprepared because of these excessive vibrations. Due to this phenomenon, it was deemed a good practice to sleep at home this night.

Midsummer, circa June 21, is the classic night for magic of all types, including household rites. This is another fire festival, so lighting a blaze on *Midsummer's Eve* and maintaining it until midnight brings luck and blessings to the house.

At one time, huge communal Midsummer fires were made. All household fires were extinguished, to be relit with a blazing brand from the Midsummer fire.

This is a fine night to dream prophetically. There are two simple processes. For the first, pick nine flowers and place them under your pillow. Lie down, calm your mind and go to sleep. The second method is simpler still: sleep with *mistletoe* under your head, and your dreams will come true. Even without flowers or herbs, your dreams should be more lucid and vivid on this night.

This is an excellent time to harvest herbs for use in magic, for their innate powers will be stronger if gathered on this day.

Cut *St. John's wort* on Midsummer's Eve and hang it in your home to guard against the effects of lightning and negativity.

If there are large rocks on your property, place flowers on the largest stone as a sacrifice to the powers of nature. (By the way, when cutting flowers for this or any other purpose, cut gently; they are forms of life. Speak to the plant and leave an offering, or perhaps a bit of energy, in payment for the part received.)

Summer brings a rush of activity away from the home, especially vacations. If you leave on an extended trip, make sure to guard the house well before you go—not only magically, but physically. All the antitheft sachets in the world won't stop a thief from entering your house through an unlocked window. Magic enhances and intensifies physical actions; it isn't a substitute for them.

Autumn rings in the harvest—in our lives as well as in the fields and gardens. At this time of year, we should be "harvesting" the fruits of our actions during the past year, reflecting and musing.

August 1 marks an ancient harvest festival date, but this date was often changed to coincide with the actual reaping schedule. *Lughnasadh*, or *Lammas* (as the Catholics renamed it in an attempt to Christianize the old Pagan festivals), was a festival of bread; thus, bread-making is traditional at this time of year.

Corn dollies—intricate figures of braided and plaited

wheat straws—are increasingly available in stores and at harvest fairs and make perfect household decorations with magical connotations. Originally, such corn dollies, or kirn babies, were made from the last sheaf of reaped wheat. The stems were braided together to make a roughly human shape—the personification of the Mother Goddess of the harvest. Such a treasure remained in the lucky house for a year, guarding it, until the dolly was destroyed and a new one fashioned.

Today, corn dollies are sold in stores. Mexico exports them to the United States, and a few craftspeople specialize in them. They can also be made at home, but as Scott learned from personal experience, this is a tough art to master.

On Lughnasadh, berry pies are traditionally baked and eaten in honor of the harvest. If your property includes a well, you can deck it with flowers or wheat stalks, for water in all forms is honored as bringer of life on this day of harvest. If you don't have a well, take a bath to which you've added a half-cup or so of grape juice or wine.

Throughout the month of August, it is supposed to be unlucky to buy a broom. Perhaps this custom was started by a lazy housekeeper.

The *Autumn Equinox*, circa September 21, marks another harvest festival. You may wish to decorate the home with dried ears of colored corn. Some folks avoid using gray corn, for it's looked upon with suspicion. But ears of red, yellow and blue corn—sacred to many North American peoples—are beautiful and inexpensive symbols of the season. Gourds and dried sheaves of wheat are also highly appropriate decorations.

Actually, these items are more than decorations. Not only do they contain specific energies which they lend to your house, they're also symbols that have powerful effects on our imaginations. When we look at the dried corn piled on the table on September 21, we're instantly aware of the significance of the day. Through the symbol, we're linked with harvest rituals of untold antiquity. Even though most of us don't grow all our food, the seasons still influence us. Magical people, as well as magical households, attune with the seasons as a part of living with nature and practicing magic.

October 31, *Samhain* or *Halloween*, is an ancient religious festival. Samhain is the old Celtic new year, so on this night the frontier between the realms of ghosts and humans is thin. Many people leave food outside, often on the porch, for the spirits of the deceased.

On this date, apples are buried in the garden, again to nourish the souls of those who have died in the past year. Perhaps in connection wth this, November 1 is the traditional start of the cider season in Britain.

After sunset on October 31, stand before a mirror and make a secret wish, visualizing it's happening. Doing this will strengthen your chances of its fulfillment.

Keep a fire lit in the fireplace all night, or a candle burning in the window. Some believe it's unlucky to leave doors or windows ajar on this night, and journeys should be finished by sunset. If clothing hangs on the line after dark, it will be imbued with strange powers, for he or she who wears it will bewitch all they meet.

For a look into the future, pull up a piece of shrubbery on this night. Put it away until Midsummer's Eve. If it's still green by then, you will have a prosperous year.

This is an excellent night for divinations and all types of psychic arts. Read the cards, scry in the crystal, throw the rune stones and look ahead at the coming 12 months.

If you do build a fire, try to burn *broom, heather* or *flax* in its flames. Although bread is a common food this time of year, don't bake any loaves on Samhain, for "ghosts" will eat it.

Thanksgiving, in late November, began when the Pilgrims planted their crops in New England later in the season than usual, so their harvest was late. Thus, the American tradition of Thanksgiving is simply a disguised and tardy harvest festival.

Hanging a bunch of ears of dried corn by their stalks on your front door before Thanksgiving ensures a prosperous, wealthy year to come.

Yule follows Thanksgiving, and so the wheel of the year is complete.

May your magical household thrive in all the seasons.

17 House Spells

Spells enjoy greater success in the magical household, so a book on the subject would be incomplete without a basic selection of house spells. Though most of these relate to the house itself, your magic needn't end there. The occult arts can help with all problems of life, and even beyond.

While using these or any other spells, remember the following basic points:

• Magic is a natural process, although forgotten by many today.

• Magic should be used only for the good of all. If you practice magic that hurts or controls others, it will rebound on you and destroy your life.

• Spells should be done with the proper visualizations. If you can't visualize well, pour your emotions and feelings into your spells. The most successful magical operations, however, are those done with both the power of emotional force and the proper visualizations to guide and direct them.

• Your home is your magic circle, your temple, your shield from negative forces, but it is also a well into which positive forces flow—forces that help power your magic.

• Spells are not sacred. This means you can change

them to suit your tastes and situations, but be careful to maintain their basic structure so that they will work.

May these spells add magic to your home.

TO PROTECT YOUR HOUSE FROM PROWLERS

Sprinkle salt throughout the house while repeating the following incantation:

> *As this salt I sprinkle about*
> *To keep the evil spirits out;*
> *Let no danger enter in*
> *Any opening herein.*
> *I now invoke the law of three*
> *This is my will, so mote it be.*

Visualize the salt creating a blanket of protective, glowing energy around your home. It is done.

TO END TIRESOME VISITS

If you have company that stays too long and interferes with your life, try some of the following spells. None of them will harm visitors; they merely impel them to leave.

Three spells involve brooms. The simplest entails nothing more than placing a broom upside down behind the door. If the guests still refuse to leave, stick a fork into the bristles of the inverted broom.

Failing this, go into a room adjoining that which the guests are in, place the broom so that its handle points toward the offending visitors and intone the following traditional rhyme:

> *Get thee hence beyond my door*
> *For I am weary to the core.*

There are other methods as well. Throwing salt on an ungracious guest's shoes (if he or she has removed them) is said to be effective, as is putting a pinch of pepper beneath

his or her chair.

Hanging a pair of scissors at the front door might also work. If not, go to the kitchen, take the pestle out of the mortar and stand it upright in the fireplace.

Tracing an equal-armed cross in the hollow of the left hand with the index finger of the right should also give your guests an urge to leave (or will at least communicate your boredom).

If none of these measures works, even when backed up with visualizations, perhaps you should try the surest spell of all—ask your visitors to leave.

FOR A PEACEFUL HOUSE

If your household is being rocked by disturbances from an outside source, gather freshly cut *parsley* from the garden (or buy fresh parsley at a store) and place it in a pan of water. Let it soak for nine minutes, then sprinkle the water throughout the house while visualizing a calm environment. Harmony should be restored.

For in-house disturbances, heat three cups of water until just boiling. Put three teaspoons of dried *valerian root* in a teapot and pour the hot water over this. Let steep 13 minutes, strain and sprinkle the mixture around the home. This should halt the strife.

HOME- AND PERSONAL-PROTECTION SPELL FOR A RENTER

Say the following while in the house:

Any evil spell against this place
Or against the one who rents it,
Will be scattered far apace
And returned to the one who sends it.
I now invoke the law of three
This is my will, so mote it be.

TO RID YOUR HOUSE OF PESTS

To clear your home of any type of insect, rodent or other household pest: On a Saturday night, three hours after sunset, make a figure of the offending creature out of wax. Place this in the infested spot and visualize the pest leaving.

To be rid of fleas: Burn a dirty dishrag the first time you hear thunder in March, or burn a handful of *fleabane* every day throughout the summer.

If you wish to drive cockroaches from your home, hold a mirror before one. It should run away in fright and never return. The catch? You must do this with each roach. A more ancient spell involving roaches is to catch a live cockroach, enclose it in a box and present it to a corpse.

An all-purpose house spell involves beating copper pans in every room of the house (including the attic, closets and basement) on the last day of February, calling out as you do:

> *Out with you, scorpions, fleas,*
> *serpents, roaches, bugs and flies*
> (or whatever is "bugging" your house)!

Now, pick up a pan with a pair of tongs and take it outside. All the bugs will obediently scurry into it, at which time you can easily dispose of them!

SATOR AMULET

Write the following ancient formula on a square piece of paper and hang it in the home. Used widely in earlier times and found among the ashes of Pompeii, it is said to guard your home against foul weather, fire and thieves.

S A T O R
A R E P O
T E N E T
O P E R A
R O T A S

TO CHANGE YOUR HOUSEHOLD LUCK

If you have terrible luck in your daily household affairs and a purification hasn't helped, try this ancient spell. Take an old spoon (it doesn't have to be clean) and walk through your house slowly, visiting each room. Visualize the spoon absorbing the house's malaise. Then walk to a crossroads and bury the spoon there. Don't look back as you return home. Things should start to perk up.

A HOUSE BLESSING

At dawn, rise and light some incense. Walk slowly through the quiet house and say the following words while visualizing their meaning and intent:

> *House of stone,*
> *metal,*
> *wood and earth;*
> *silent one,*
> *protective one,*
> *you of the four winds;*
> *house of health,*
> *wealth,*
> *joy and peace;*
> *guardian,*
> *sustainer,*
> *you of the Earth;*
> *house of stone,*
> *metal,*
> *wood and earth,*
> *secure one,*
> *peaceful one,*
> *you of the charm:*
> *guarded and protected you be,*
> *cleansed and pure you be,*
> *peaceful and loving you be.*
> *It is finished in beauty.*
> *It is finished in beauty,*
> *it is finished in beauty.*

Set down the incense and draw as exact a likeness of your house as you can from your imagination. Draw it from all angles: from above, from the front, from behind. If you live in an apartment, draw the building as well.

When finished, go outside and check your drawing. Is it as accurate as you can make it? If not, draw a new one or make changes until the drawing satisfies you. No great skill is required; you need only make a recognizable likeness of your home.

When finished, take a white candle and a sharp knife. Cut seven evenly spaced notches in the candle so that you create a knobbed candle. Now set the drawing down on a table where it can remain for seven days. Set the candle on top of it and light it while visualizing your home as blessed, safe and loving.

Let the candle burn down one notch the first day as you go about your early morning business, then pinch or snuff out the flame and leave it until the next day. The next morning, repeat the ritual—from lighting the incense and saying the blessing chant to burning one candle notch.

On the seventh day, after the candle has burned down all the way, fold the drawing into a tight package and secure it with red or white cord. Place it in a wooden box with salt and dried roses and tie the box firmly shut with another white cord. Finally, place the box in the home where it won't be seen or found.

SPELLS TO GUARD CHILDREN

There are untold thousands of spells for guarding children. Though the child's presence in the home should be protection enough, anxious parents through the ages have evolved a number of further guards.

In Wales, babies were dressed in clothing that featured knotted red ribbons. Red, the color of life, was thought to ward off its opposite, and the knots tied up evil.

Cradles have their own strange lore and magic. According to ancient belief, anyone who rocks an empty cradle will soon fill it. Babies lying helpless in cradles are protected by red threads tied to the cradle. Peoples living along the Rio Grande placed an ear of corn alongside the infant to shield it from supernatural forces, while a steel key or piece of stale bread similarly guarded the child.

To prevent children from wandering away from home, they were taken outside and shown the house, solemnly, completely. Once this was done, the children wouldn't unthinkingly walk away from it, and the parents could rest easily.

Older children were guarded by necklaces of seashells, which would also imbue them with love, wealth and productiveness in their later lives.

Any of the protective bed spells can be utilized for children since they are often subject to ills, from nightmares to physical illness, during the night.

Magic performed with and for children, especially protective magic, should never replace sound safety practices. As soon as your children are able to do so, have them memorize your phone number, address and family name. Counsel them on common practices—don't open the door to strangers, don't accept rides from "friendly" people, and so on. Again, magic works only when backed up with physical efforts.

Since you know your child best, try creating personalized protective spells and charms, perhaps drawing the whole family into the process. Where they are present, children are an important part of the magical household.

OTHER SPELLS FOR CHILDREN

Teddy bears, named after President Theodore Roosevelt, are still considered luck-bringing talismans for children. You might wish to increase a bear's influence by saying a protective chant over it before presenting it to the child.

An ideal spell for children involves kites. If it's windy outside and a child is sick, depressed or anxious about a problem, buy or make a kite with the child. While making it, "pour" the child's problem into the kite. (If willing or able, the child should participate in this process.) Once the kite has been made or assembled, have the child fly it. As the kite dips and sways, it will release the child's illness or problem into the element of Air.

18   Household Omens and Portents

Let your furniture predict your future? The idea may sound strange, but for centuries—from Babylonian times and even earlier—household objects and occurrences have been prized for glimpses of future events.

Many of these ancient ideas are odd, alien or amusing, but they do reflect the sacredness of all existence in early times. You could trudge over to the seer or stand in line to visit the Oracle at Delphi—or you could watch your furniture.

For instance, if you are rocking in your rocking chair and it starts to move along the floor, company will show on your porch before nighttime. A chair that rocks by itself signifies the imminent arrival of bad news.

If you knock your chair over when rising from the table, it is a sign that you lied while seated there. Turning a chair on one leg so that it pivots usually presages a household fight.

Any large piece of wooden furniture—such as a wardrobe, table or chest—that starts to dry out and crack is signaling a change in the weather.

If you are dreaming away one night and suddenly feel like the world's falling, perhaps one of the slats of your bed

155

has fallen out. If so, don't worry; this is a sign that riches will soon be coming your way. Also concerning beds, climbing out of bed over the footboard when first rising in the morning portends a fortunate day.

The kitchen has its share of portents, too. If apples burst while baking in the oven, good news is on the way for the cook. Eggs that crack while boiling are a sign that visitors are expected.

Many people around the world abhor Americans' bland, precooked rice. Real rice sticks to itself; it has a different texture. When this type of rice forms a ring around the edge of the pot while cooking, the cook will become rich.

Knocking over the sugar bowl is another sign of money, probably harkening back to the days when sugar was prohibitively expensive. Spilling pepper signifies a coming fight, while upsetting the salt shaker is a well-known signal of trouble. Throw a pinch of pepper or salt over the left shoulder to avoid the hex.

Accidentally mixing up salt and sugar in a recipe is a sweet sign, regardless of the taste of the finished dish. It presages good news. Forgetting to add spices while cooking not only decreases the flavor of your food, it also signifies trouble ahead. Remedy this by adding the spices as soon as possible.

Bubbles in your morning coffee presage money. If they are near the side of the cup you drink from, the money will come soon; if on the far side, it will come more slowly.

If you drink tea, look into your cup. Floating tea leaves signify money coming your way. The tea leaves themselves, of course, can be read to foretell the future. Get a good book on the subject or simply look at the patterns the leaves make and let your psychic powers flow.

There are some kitchen portents of approaching rain. If you must add a lot of water to boiling food, showers will descend. If the coffeepot boils over more often than usual, this is also a sign of impending precipitation.

Many omens emerge at the dining table. Crossing knives while setting the table foretells long journeys, while a piece of bread falling from someone's hand means a beggar will soon be knocking at the door. (This doesn't necessarily mean a ramshackle, bearded bum, though; it could be a friend who's low on cash.)

Spilling water on the tablecloth, by right of sympathetic magic, indicates that rain is on the way. If you drop a glass and it doesn't break, this is proof that you have friends who would go through fire for you.

Silverware dropped at the table indicates the impending arrival of a visitor—a fork represents a man, a spoon a woman. Dropping a knife also means a visitor—if the blade sticks into the floor.

Animals are frequently watched to predict the future. A bird flying into a house for no apparent reason is a sign of good luck and fortune for the owner (but perhaps not for the bird). It may also portend news from a distance.

Swallows settling in at your home mean that it will never want for luck. The same is true of martins. If you hear a mockingbird while falling asleep, good luck will be yours.

Snakes were once kept as household guardians, and a snake in the home is still considered lucky. If a snake crawls up your doorsteps, it may mean that someone from another country will enter your house. A snake in the garden also brings good fortune.

Wild animal tracks in the snow, completely encircling the house, are another sign of good luck.

Seeing a spider in the house in the morning, or anytime, is good luck; killing one brings bad luck. A spider or bee entering your home through an open window indicates news on the way.

Doors opening by themselves signal the impending arrival of company. Cracks in the ceiling and soot dropping from the chimney indicate bad weather ahead. A falling picture presages a journey for someone in the family.

If a broom drops across a doorway, you will soon go on a journey. (Make sure to pick it up quickly; don't step over it.) When your cupboard doors are left open, people will gossip about you.

If your garden gate bangs open and shut at night, you will have many visitors the next day. And finally, if the doorbell rings and you don't answer it, you will lose a friend. (This was probably invented by traveling salesmen and bill collectors.)

19 The Household Altar

Magic and religion are coming home. Today, many people are turning away from orthodox faiths to embrace half-forgotten beliefs from around the world. Ancient religions and magical systems are experiencing popular revivals. Dogma and structure are being left behind in favor of new forms of religious expression. Accompanying this change has been a renaissance of folk magic, with many people investigating ancient magical practices and using them to improve their lives.

Followers of these ways often practice them at home, for there are few thriving temples dedicated to Athena or Marduk, and not all of us have the Serpent Mound or Stonehenge in our backyards.

Fortunately, the home can be an ideal place for acts of magic and expressions of faith. Surrounded by familiar energies, magic and spirituality flow. Many prefer to stay close to the home fires when communing with their deities or conjuring up healing energy; there they feel comfortable, safe and secure.

In some households, a particular room is devoted to magic and religious pursuits; in others, the whole house is the "temple." Perhaps most often, some type of home altar is created at which rites can take place.

Household altars have ancient predecessors. At times, the home altar was dedicated to the "official" state religion. More often, it was the site of reverence for household spirits, ancestral or localized deities and now-forgotten goddesses and gods of the trees, stars, fruits, animals and elements.

These altars were often simple. Among the common forms were a cleared space of ground marked out with stones, shells or colored sand; a tree stump; a small shrine set in the garden, and a niche in the wall. Images of the deities were often placed there, with bowls or plates to hold offerings left daily by the religious householders.

Though this chapter is titled "The Household Altar," the whole house can be seen as an altar to the deities of life. The foundation is the altar's base, the hearth its sacred fire, the windows shining candles and the garden its offering of fruits and flowers. Those who walk its floors "worship" life.

You may wish to create a simple altar for your home. This need not be for strictly religious purposes; it is often utilized solely for magic, or for other spiritual practices such as meditation.

Indeed, you may see your home altar simply as a power center, the heart of the house, keeping it running smoothly through bad times as well as blessed.

You may be concerned about disguising your altar. With a little discretion, it can pass as a collection of curious objects or an off-beat decorative piece. If you must hide your altar, try setting it up inside a drawer, in a closet (be careful when using flames) or in a bedroom corner.

The ideal arrangement is a permanent altar, one that never has to be dismantled. Altars work best if allowed to sit quietly, undisturbed, when not in use. They should be centrally located, easily accessible and situated in a place that

feels "right." If this isn't possible, simply set up the altar each time you feel the need to use it, then put it away.

Since this is a highly personal subject, only you can determine which objects to place on your altar. If you belong to an organized religion or follow a faith with specific symbols and deities, you might place symbols or images related to your faith on the altar. This will connect your home with the energies of your spiritual practices. A Wiccan, for example, might include a statue of a Moon goddess on her altar.

Fire, in any form, is a frequent addition to altars, for it has long been revered as sacred. Candles are quite appropriate, as are their antecedents, oil lamps. Candles in glass jars—often called "seven-day" candles—are ideal for altar use. They can be left burning for several days with relative safety and are available in a wide range of colors, making them useful for their symbolic meanings.

White candles are often left burning continuously on household altars to promote spirituality and peace within the home as well as to honor deity. Use the colors that seem right. (See Chapter 2 for candle colors and their household influences.)

Charms, amulets and personal-power objects also can be placed on the altar. Favorite stones, shells gathered on distant beaches or any other objects that you feel are special and important belong on the altar as well. Many of the charms mentioned in this book are perfect for altar use.

If you decide that a pile of fossils will guard your home like nothing else, add them to your altar, where their powers will be enhanced.

Choose objects that have special meanings to you, that are related to the house (tiny brooms, pieces of brick, a picture of the structure) or that are magically potent (four-leaf clovers, feathers, coral or turquoise).

In some parts of the world to this day such altars are decked with flowers, greens or fruit, which are cut with simple thanks to the plant providing the sacrifice. The flowers and leaves may be fashioned into garlands, wreaths or leis. Any seasonal flowers that you enjoy can be added to the altar to increase its powers and appearance. These are seen as sacrifices to the energies, but are also admired for their beauty.

Salt is often present on the altar as well, in a box, bag, bottle or cut-crystal jar. It cleanses and purifies the altar and also lends it the power to prevent poverty and financial misfortune.

Incense burners, another common altar object, provide a convenient means of honoring the divine. Lighting incense daily and placing it in the burner not only "pleases" the gods, it also clears the house of stuffy vibrations.

Burning incense regularly is a highly recommended magical household practice.* Perhaps the best incense for daily use is the joss-stick type, which can easily be lit and placed in a bowl of sand or an incense burner. Choose incenses not only for their scents, but also for their powers and influences, as described here:

Almond: wisdom
Cedar: purification, money, healing
Cherry: love
Cinnamon: spirituality, healing, protection
Coconut: purification, relaxation, lessened sexual drive
Frankincense: spirituality, protection, exorcism
Gardenia: healing, spirituality, love, peace
Jasmine: love, luck, money

---

* See *The Magic of Incense, Oil and Brews*, Cunningham (Llewellyn).

164 / Magical Household

Lemon: purification, love
Lotus: spirituality, protection
Musk: passion, courage
Myrrh: spirituality, protection, healing, exorcism
Patchouli: love, passion, money
Pine: purification, money, protection
Rose: love, healing, protection, luck
Sandalwood: spirituality, protection, healing
Vanilla: love

If available, cone or block incense can be burned, but it is usually so heavily cut with base that the original scent is lost. The same is true of stick incense. Try several different brands until you find one you like.

Raw or ground incense is burned on a charcoal block made especially for this purpose (not the charcoal intended for barbecues). Such blocks are placed in censers or cauldrons, usually on the altar. The block is lit and sputters until it glows red. Incense is then sprinkled onto it. This is ideal if you wish to fumigate your home, for the charcoal sends up clouds of smoke.

You can make incenses using the following recipes or design your own. All ingredients should be ground to a powder before blending. Though many homemade incenses don't smell as sweet as the artificially scented commercial sticks and cones, they are much more powerful. Following are a few basic recipes for home use.

House Purification Incense

Cedar—1 part
Sandalwood—1 part
Myrrh—1 part

Grind, mix and burn in the house when needed.

Simple Household Purification Incense

Sandalwood—1 part
Cinnamon—1 part

Grind together in the mortar and burn as needed.

Health Incense

Myrrh—2 parts
Sage—1 part
Rosemary—1 part
Sandalwood—2 parts

Burn when there is illness in the house.

House Wealth Incense

A pinch of household dust
Frankincense—3 parts
Myrrh—1 part
Patchouli—1 part
Allspice, nutmeg and ginger combined—1/2 part

Grind together, burn every Thursday before a mirror.

Protection Incense

Basil—1/2 part
Frankincense—1 part
Myrrh—1 part
Pine—1 part
Sage—1/2 part

Grind together, burn when needed.

If you are a practitioner of magic, you may want to place your ritual tools and objects—drum, rattle, magic blades, crystals, cords, wand and pentacles—on the altar.

All will be intimately linked with the house's well-being and spiritual current.

Aligning the altar with the four elements is a common practice. The elements are the sum of the universal forces divided into four basic types of energies. Invoking their presence in your home lends it their specific powers.

A fragrant bloom, feather or smoking censer can represent the element of *Air*, which brings intelligence and organization to the home.

The element of *Fire* is symbolized by a burning candle, an oil lamp or a chunk of volcanic rock, such as obsidian, olivine or lava. Fire blesses the home with warmth, passion, energy, protection and health.

A dish of water or some quartz crystal signifies the element of *Water*, which brings love, contentment, spirituality, psychism and a sense of family unity to the home.

Finally, a bowl of earth, a clay pot, a pile of stones or a container of salt tunes in the element of *Earth*. This element lends your home stability, physical strength, a nurturing atmosphere, money and food.

One object for each of the four elements can be placed on the altar to bring these influences into your home.

A "household guardian" is an ideal addition to the altar. In essence, this is a magically produced thought-form or concentration of energies, created through ritual, which guards and protects the house and those who live in it.

Such a guardian usually "resides" in a physical object—a rock, statue, jar or other item—that will be put to no other use and that can be moved with you if you ever leave the house.

A household guardian can be created in several ways. Let's say you own a statue of a Viking, for example. Place it on the altar between shining white candles. In your mind, create a picture of this guardian: a sword-slashing bar-

barian, loyal only to you and your friends; a goddess of such intense power that a wave of her wand dissuades all who would harm or injure the house; or a soldier of fortune with a shell-spitting machine gun. Gaze at the object while visualizing this guardian. Now infuse it with a personality— stern, commanding, loving, gentle but firm.

You must *see* this guardian you're creating and *know* that it will protect your home. Now address it in words, images or gestures. Coax it into the object. Give it explicit instructions. For example: "Protect this house and all who live within it. Allow no one with envious, destructive or dangerous motives to enter. Grow in power."

Once the object is fully charged with the guardian, keep it in a prominent place in the house. A permanent altar is ideal, if you have one, or near the front entrance, the dining room or the bedroom.

Give the guardian additional power by daily remind- ing it of its duties, and it should serve you well. If you move from the house, take the guardian with you to your new place and shift its attention toward its new home.

How your altar fits into your house and life depends on you. You may visit it every morning upon rising, light the candles, meditate for a few moments, then quench the flames and go on with your daily life. Or you may visit it once a week to work a spell or say a prayer.

One word of warning, however: A household altar re- flects the altar-tender as well as the type of home in which it resides. If your altar is dirty, messy or unkempt, clean it and get your house back together. Keeping your altar shining and bright will aid you in creating a truly magical house- hold.

If you fashion such an altar, call upon the powers or deities to bless and guard your home. Infuse it with posi- tive, magical, uplifting vibrations. Swirl incense smoke and attune.

The household altar can become the magical focus of a home, but this isn't the ideal. *All aspects* of the home and life within it are magical. Strive to see this reality.

Whether you believe we naturally evolved or were placed here on some divine being's whim, living itself is a sacred act. Treat your life, home and loved ones with reverence, and reverence will be radiated back to you.

The magical heritage of a house is rich and of infinite variety. In practicing this ancient magic, we link with our predecessors and the powers they touched—those of the Earth, of Nature and of Life itself.

May your home be magical indeed!

GLOSSARY

Amulet: an object worn, carried or placed to dispel or drive away negativity or other vibrations; a protective object.

Astral Projection: the practice of separating the consciousness from the physical body so that the former may move about unhindered by time, space or gravity.

Bane: that which destroys life; more broadly, all negativity, from evil thoughts to physical attacks.

Banish: to drive away evil, negativity, spirits.

Besom: broom.

Censer: a heat-proof vessel in which incense is burned; an incense burner.

Corn Dolly: a construction of plaited, dried stalks of grain (usually wheat, rye, barley, oats, etc.), often human-shaped, representing the fertility of the Earth and the Goddess. Once braided from the last sheaves reaped at the end of the harvest, corn dollies aren't made from cobs or husks; the word "corn" originally referred to any grain other than maize.

Curse: a concentration of negative or destructive energy, deliberately formed and directed toward a person, place or thing.

Divination: the art of obtaining knowledge through the use of tools that either point to future events or stimulate psychic powers within the user.

Elements, the: Earth, Air, Fire and Water. These four essences are the building blocks of the universe. Everything that exists (or has the potential to exist) contains one or more of these energies. The elements are also "at large" in the world and within ourselves and can be utilized to cause change through magic.

Evil Eye, the: the supposed glance capable of causing great harm—even death—that was once almost universally feared.

Exorcism: the act of removing negative forces or entities, usually from a place or object (rarely from a person).

Infusion: an herbal tea; once called a potion. Recipes differ, but infusions are usually made by steeping two teaspoons of dried herb in a cup of hot water.

Magic: the process of causing needed change through the use of natural but little-understood powers. Magic is a *natural* process; there is nothing supernatural about it. Since it is a largely forgotten or forsaken art today, it is widely ridiculed as well as feared. But it's still here.

Pentagram: a five-pointed star used in magic for centuries. The pentagram represents the four elements plus the fifth, Spirit or *Akasha*. It also symbolizes the human body, the five senses and the hand. It is most often used in protective magic.

Scry, to: to gaze into a shiny or clear object—such as a fire, a pool of ink, or a crystal ball—to awaken and summon psychic powers.

Shaman: a man or woman who has obtained knowledge

of other dimensions as well as of the Earth, usually through periods of alternate states of consciousness. This knowledge lends the shaman the power to change the world through magic. Shamans were once referred to as "witch doctors," but the latter term has fallen into deserved disfavor, and today shamans have even gained respect as psychologists and botanical healers.

Shamanism: the practice of shamans, usually ritualistic or magical in nature but rarely truly "religious." Shamanism isn't priest-craft; it's magic-craft. Perhaps the term "nature-magic" would serve as an apt description.

Sun Wheel: an ancient solar symbol (also known as the Flyfot Cross). It was sacred to Vishnu, the beneficent Hindu God of Life, was known and used in Iceland before the year 1000 and was also used as an amulet against the evil eye all over the globe in ancient times, including Scotland, Greece, Sicily, Malta, Japan, Mycenae, Troy, North America and throughout Europe. Later, it acquired a negative reputation because of Hitler's unfortunate use of the *svastika* (Sanskrit) as a symbol for his new order. It was a common symbol until comparatively recent times in rugs, jewelry and other items before it was tainted. In the United States, it was and still is used in Pennsylvania Dutch hex magic as a protective symbol designed to deflect or disperse negative energies.

Sympathetic Magic: the art of physically imitating or acting out the goal of magic, used with ritual. The imitation serves to properly channel the energies used in magic.

Trilithon: a grouping of stones in which two are upright and one lies on top of them, forming an archway. England's Stonehenge contains the most famous trilithons.

Visualization: the art of forming mental images or pictures that are magically utilized to direct energy and bring the visualized need into manifestation.

Wicca: a contemporary religion with spiritual roots in prehistory. Wicca worships the life-force of the universe as personified by a Goddess and a God. Until recently, it was almost always referred to as "Witchcraft."

Witch: a female or male practitioner of natural magic, spells and herbal knowledge; a person who works with the elements and with more "earthy" magics of the everyday folk; also used to describe members of Wicca.

Witch Bottle: a bottle or jar containing herbs, shards of glass and other objects, designed to protect a person or place (such as a house). It is often buried or placed in a window. In the past, all sorts of disagreeable things were added to Witch bottles, which were sometimes used by the ignorant to destroy the powers of a suspected "Witch"—hence the name.

Witchcraft: the practice of natural magic—magic using herbs, stones and candles; spell-casting; beneficent magic. Also used to refer to the religion of Wicca.

BIBLIOGRAPHY

Alderman, Clifford Lindsey. *Symbols of Magic.* Julian Messner, New York, 1977.

Baker, Margaret. *Gardener's Magic and Folklore.* Universe, New York, 1978.

Baker, Margaret. *Folklore and Customs of Rural England.* Rowman and Littlefield, Totowa, N.J., 1974.

Bowness, Charles. *The Witch's Gospel.* Robert Hale, London, 1979.

Budge, E. A. Wallis. *Amulets and Talismans.* University Books, New Hyde Park, N.Y., 1968.

Burkhardt, V. R. *Chinese Creeds and Customs.* Four volumes bound as one. Golden Mountain Publishers, Taipei, China, 1971 (?).

Chappell, Helen. *The Waxing Moon: A Gentle Guide to Magick.* Links, New York, 1974.

Childe, Gordon. *What Happened in History.* Pelican, Baltimore, 1969.

Cirlot, J. E. *A Dictionary of Symbols.* Philosophical Library, New York, 1962.

Coffin, Tristram P. and Henning Cohen, eds. *Folklore from the Working Folk of America.* Anchor, Garden City, N.Y., 1970.

Coffin, Tristram P., and Henning Cohen, eds. *Folklore in America.* Anchor, Garden City, N.Y., 1970.

Cowan, Lore. *Are You Superstitious?* Pocket Books, New York, 1970.

173

Cunningham, Scott. *Earth Power*. Llewellyn Publications, St.Paul, 1983.

Cunningham, Scott. *Magical Herbalism*. Llewellyn Publications, St. Paul, 1982.

Cunningham, Scott. *Cunningham's Encyclopedia of Magical Herbs*. Llewellyn Publications, St. Paul, 1985.

Daniels, Cora Linn, ed. *Encyclopedia of Superstitions, Folklore and the Occult Sciences of the World*. Three volumes. Gale Research Co., Detroit, 1971.

DeLys, Claudia. *A Treasury of American Superstitions*. Philosophical Library, New York, 1948.

Denning, Melita and Osborne Phillips. *The Llewellyn Practical Guide to Astral Projection*. Llewellyn Publications, St. Paul, 1979.

Fielding, William J. *Strange Superstitions and Magical Practices*. Paperback Library, New York, 1966.

Garfield, Patricia. *Creative Dreaming*. Ballantine, New York, 1976.

Gregor, Arthur A. *Amulets, Talismans and Fetishes*. Scribner's, New York, 1975.

Hand, Wayland, Anna Casetta and Sondra B. Theiderman, eds. *Popular Beliefs and Superstitions: A Compendium of American Folklore*. Three volumes. G. K. Hall, Boston, 1981.

Howells, William. *Back of History*. Anchor, New York, 1963.

Jayne, Walter Addison. *The Healing Gods of Ancient Civilizations*. University Books, New Hyde Park, N.Y., 1962.

Johnson, Clifford. *What They Say in New England*. Columbia University, New York, 1963.

Jones, T. Gwynn. *Welsh Folklore and Folk Customs*. D. S. Brewer, Cambridge, 1979.

Kittredge, George Lyman. *Witchcraft in Old and New England*. Russell and Russell, New York, 1956.

Knowlson, T. Sharper. *The Origins of Popular Superstitions and Customs.* T. Werner Laurie, Ltd., London, 1910.

Krythe, Maymie. *All About the Months.* Harper and Row, New York, 1966.

Leach, Maria. *The Soup Stone: The Magic of Familiar Things.* Mayflower, London, 1954.

Leach, Maria, ed. *The Standard Dictionary of Folklore, Mythology and Legend.* Funk and Wagnalls, New York, 1972.

Leek, Sybil. *The Night Voyagers: You and Your Dreams.* Mason/Charter, New York, 1975.

Masse, Henri. *Persian Beliefs and Customs.* Human Relations Area Files, New Haven, 1954.

Maple, Eric. *Superstition and the Superstitious.* A. S. Barnes, Cranbury, N.J., 1972.

Mickaharic, Draja. *Spiritual Cleansing.* Samuel Weiser, York Beach, Me., 1982.

Norris, David and Jacquemine Charrott-Lodwidge. *The Book of Spells.* Fireside, New York, 1974.

Randolph, Vance. *Ozark Superstitions.* Columbia University, New York, 1947.

Rossbach, Sarah. *Feng Shui: The Chinese Art of Placement.* Dutton, New York, 1983.

St. Leger-Gordon, Ruth E. *Witchcraft and Folklore of Dartmoor.* Scribner's, New York, 1978.

Sarnoff, June and Reynold Ruffins. *Take Warning! A Book of Superstitions.* Scribner's, New York, 1972.

Saxon, Lyle. *Gumbo Ya-Ya.* HoughtonMifflin, Boston, 1945.

Simmons, Marc. *Witchcraft in the Southwest: Spanish and Indian Supernaturalism on the Rio Grande.* The University of Nebraska Press, Lincoln, Neb., 1980.

Tallman, Marjorie. *Dictionary of American Folklore.* Philosophical Library, New York, 1959.

Valente, Doreen. *An ABC of Witchcraft Past and Present.* St. Martin's, New York, 1973.

Waring, Phillipa. *A Dictionary of Omens and Superstitions.* Ballantine, New York, 1979.

Whitlock, Ralph. *The Folklore of Devon.* Rowman and Littlefield, Totowa, N.J., 1977.

INDEX

V

T

STAY IN TOUCH

On the following pages you will find listed, with their current prices, some of the books and tapes now available on related subjects. Your book dealer stocks most of these, and will stock new titles in the Llewellyn series as they become available. We urge your patronage.

However, to obtain our full catalog, to keep informed of new titles as they are released and to benefit from informative articles and helpful news, you are invited to write for our bi-monthly news magazine/catalog. A sample copy is free, and it will continue coming to you at no cost as long as you are an active mail customer. Or you may keep it coming for a full year with a donation of just $2.00 in U.S.A. ($7.00 for Canada & Mexico, $20.00 overseas, first class mail). Many bookstores also have *The Llewellyn New Times* available to their customers. Ask for it.

Stay in touch! In *The Llewellyn New Times'* pages you will find news and reviews of new books, tapes and services, announcements of meetings and seminars, articles helpful to our readers, news of authors, advertising of products and services, special money-making opportunities, and much more.

The Llewellyn New Times
P.O. Box 64383-Dept. 124, St. Paul, MN 55164-0383, U.S.A.

•　　　•　　　•

TO ORDER BOOKS AND TAPES

If your book dealer does not have the books and tapes described on the following pages readily available, you may order them direct from the publisher by sending full price in U.S. funds, plus $1.00 for handling and 50¢ each book or item for postage within the United States; outside USA surface mail add $1.00 extra per item. Outside USA air mail add $7.00 per item.

FOR GROUP STUDY AND PURCHASE

Because there is a great deal of interest in group discussion and study of the subject matter of this book, we feel that we should encourage the adoption and use of this particular book by such groups by offering a special "quantity" price to group leaders or "agents".

Our Special Quality Price for a minimum order of five copies of THE MAGICAL HOUSEHOLD is $23.85 Cash-With-Order. This price includes postage and handling within the United States. Minnesota residents must add 6% sales tax. For additional quantities, please order in multiples of five. For Canadian and foreign orders, add postage and handling charges as above. Credit Card (VISA, MasterCard, American Express, Diners' Club) Orders are accepted. Charge Card Orders only may be phoned free ($15.00 minimum order) within the U.S.A. by dialing 1-800-THE MOON (in Canada call: 1-800-FOR-SELF). Customer Service calls dial 1-612-291-1970 and ask for "Kae." Mail Orders to:

LLEWELLYN PUBLICATIONS
P.O. Box 64383-Dept. 124 / St. Paul, MN 55164-0383, U.S.A.

EARTH POWER: TECHNIQUES OF NATURAL MAGIC
by Scott Cunningham

Magic is the art of working with the forces of Nature to bring about necessary, and desired, changes. The forces of Nature—expressed through Earth, Air, Fire and Water—are our "spiritual ancestors" who paved the way for our emergence from the pre-historic seas of creation. Attuning to, and working with these energies in magic not only lends you the power to affect changes in your life, it also allows you to sense your own place in the larger scheme of Nature. Using the "Old Ways" enables you to live a better life, and to deepen your understanding of the world about you. The tools and powers of magic are around you, waiting to be grasped and utilized. This book gives you the means to put Magic into your life, shows you how to make and use the tools, and gives you spells for every purpose.

0-87542-121-0, 250 pages, illus., softcover.   **$6.95**

MAGICAL HERBALISM—The Secret Craft of the Wise
by Scott Cunningham

In magical herbalism, certain plants are prized for the special range of energies—the vibrations, or powers—they possess. Magical herbalism unites the powers of plants and man to produce, and direct, change in accord with human will and desire.

This is the Magic of amulets and charms, sachets and herbal pillows, incenses and scented oils, simples and infusions and anointments. It's Magic as old as our knowledge of plants, an art that anyone can learn and practice, and once again enjoy as we look to the Earth to rediscover our roots and make inner connections with the world of Nature.

This is Magic that is beautiful and natural—a Craft of Hand and Mind merged with the Power and Glory of Nature: a special kind that does not use the medicinal powers of herbs, but rather the subtle vibrations and scents that touch the psychic centers and stir the astral field in which we live to work at the causal level behind the material world.

This is the Magic of Enchantment . . . of word and gesture to shape the images of mind and channel the energies of the herbs. It is a Magic for *everyone*—for the herbs are easily and readily obtained, the tools are familiar or easily made, and the technology that of home and garden.

This book includes step-by-step guidance to the preparation of herbs and to their compounding in incense and oils, sachets and amulets, simples and infusions, with simple rituals and spells for every purpose.

0-87542-120-2, 243 pages, 5¼ x 8, illus., softcover.   **$7.95**

CUNNINGHAM'S ENCYCLOPEDIA OF MAGICAL HERBS
by Scott Cunningham

This is an expansion on the material presented in his first Llewellyn book, *Magical Herbalism*. This is not just another herbal for medicinal uses of herbs; this is the most comprehensive source of herbal data for magical uses. Each of the over 400 herbs are illustrated and the magical properties, planetary rulerships, genders, deities, folk and Latin names are given. There is a large annotated bibliography, a list of mail order suppliers, a folk name cross reference, and all the herbs are fully indexed. No other book like it exists. Find out what herbs to use for luck, love, success, money, divination, astral projection and much more. Fun, interesting and fully illustrated with unusual woodcuts from old herbals.

0-87542-122-9, 6 x 9, 350 pages, illus., softcover. $12.95

CUNNINGHAM'S ENCYCLOPEDIA OF CRYSTAL, GEM AND METAL MAGIC by Scott Cunningham

It is very rare that a book becomes a classic. Books on New Age topics must not only report the truth, but capture the minds and hearts of people all over the world. Just such a book is *CUNNINGHAM'S ENCYCLOPEDIA OF CRYSTAL, GEM AND METAL MAGIC.*

Here you will find the most complete information anywhere on the magical qualities of over 75 crystals and gemstones as well as several metals. The information includes:

•The Energy of Each Gem, Crystal or Metal•The Planet(s) Which Rule(s) the Crystal, Gem or Metal•The Magical Element (Air, Earth, Fire, Water) Associated with the Gem, Crystal or Metal• The Deities Associated with Each•The Tarot Card Associated with Each•The Magical Powers each Crystal, Metal and Stone are believed to Possess•

ALSO INCLUDED IS A COMPLETE DESCRIPTION OF HOW TO USE EACH GEMSTONE, CRYSTAL AND METAL FOR MAGICAL PURPOSES.

This is the book everyone will want to have! This is the book everyone will be quoting. This will be the classic on the subject.

0-87542-126-1, illustrated, 8 color plates, softbound. $12.95

THE MAGIC OF INCENSE, OILS AND BREWS
by Scott Cunningham

Many of the recipes used by the wise ones of old for the making of special incenses, oils, brews, ointments, sachets, etc. have been lost or have been such closely guarded secrets that until now, no one knew exactly how to make them. Scott Cunningham has researched this area well and has described and explained in detail exactly how to prepare and use over 125 different incenses, 60 oils, 15 magical ointments, 15 herb baths, 10 magical brews, 15 sachets, 8 magical inks and more! These recipes come primarily from European sources and are *not* the ones you will find in other sources on magical workings. Some are original, some come from very old manuscripts, some were passed down from teachers and some are indeed ancient.

0-87542-123-7, 192 pages, illus., softcover.   **$6.95**

LLEWELLYN GEM•BAG

Llewellyn's Gem•Bag is an attractive suede drawstring pouch containing 13 different polished gemstones for healing, well-being, and good luck. Each stone has its own special energy, its unique energies and vibrations from its place of origin. They share their gifts and energies with you.Each of these medicine bags comes with complete instructions and descriptions of the gems. Gems include: Amazonite, Amethyst, Aventurine, Blue Lace Agate, Carnelian, Crazy Lace Agate, Jade, Moonstone, Petrified Wood, Rhodonite, Rose Quartz, Apache Tear Drop, Snowflake Obsidian, Tiger Eye, and Unikite.

GEM•BAG   **$9.95 each**

LLEWELLYN'S QUARTZ CRYSTALS

Beautiful natural quartz crystals. Llewellyn now has a good supply of crystals that were mined in Arkansas. They come in two sizes and are high-energy crystals. They are all single terminated and are clear at the point. We look them over before we send them to you so you are guaranteed of getting one of the finest crystals available.

Crystal A, approx. 2 inches long $10.00 + $1.00 postage
Crystal B, approx. 3½ inches long $17.00 + $1.50 postage

LLEWELLYN'S GEMSTONES

Healers and magicians have always used special stones in their work. We are now offering some of these special stones, each endowed by legend and ancient tradition with specific powers.

GEM•PAK I contains one each of the following four stones: Amethyst, Bloodstone, Carnelian, and Tiger Eye.

GEM•PAK II contains one each of the following four stones: Rose Quartz, Lace Agate, Sodalite, and Apache Tear Drop.

GEM•CARD contains Amethyst, Bloodstone, Tiger Eye, Carnelian, Smoky Quartz, Aventurine, Rose Quartz, Apache Tear Drop, Tourmalinated Quartz, Sodalite.

GEM•PAK I / $5.00   GEM•PAK II / $5.00   GEM•CARD / $7.95